SCHILLER AND BURNS

KU-774-005

MODERN LANGUAGE STUDIES

J. Boyd, J. Seznec, P. E. Russell, *General Editors*

SCHILLER AND BURNS

and Other Essays

BY

WILLIAM WITTE

PROFESSOR OF GERMAN IN THE UNIVERSITY OF ABERDEEN

BASIL BLACKWELL

OXFORD

1959

© *Basil Blackwell & Mott, Ltd., 1959*

First printed in 1959

Printed in Great Britain for BASIL BLACKWELL & MOTT, LIMITED
by A. R. MOWBRAY & CO. LIMITED in the City of Oxford
and bound at the KEMP HALL BINDERY

TO MY WIFE

'. . . a Domino autem proprie uxor prudens.'

PREFACE

THE essays in this volume centre round Schiller, whose works and personality have continued to engage my attention since I published a monograph on him ten years ago. Apart from being rewarding in itself, the subject—whatever Schiller's detractors may say—is, and is likely to remain, of crucial importance in the field of German literary studies. It also has a close bearing on present-day life and thought. A recent collection of speeches commemorating the 150th anniversary of Schiller's death—*Schiller: Reden im Gedenk-jahr 1955*[1]—provides striking proof of this contemporary relevance.

The essay on 'Goethe and *Ius Naturale*' might at first sight appear extraneous to the main theme of this book. It is being included because it links up with the observations on 'Law and the Social Order in Schiller's Thought' which precede it. Read together, the two essays demonstrate the prevalence of Natural Law concepts in eighteenth-century German literature and indicate some of their implications. The concluding essay on 'Carlyle as a Critic of German Literature' ranges rather more widely than the rest, though Schiller naturally comes within its scope.

There remains the agreeable duty of acknowledging various obligations. Like my earlier book on Schiller (Blackwell's Modern Language Studies, 1949) and my edition of *Wallenstein* (Blackwell's German Texts, 1952), this volume has benefited by Professor J. Boyd's shrewd editorial guidance, and I am, as ever, grateful for his sustained and friendly interest in my work. To Sir Basil Blackwell I am no less deeply indebted for advice and encouragement: I count it a privilege to have this collection of Schiller studies published under his imprint.

Nowadays a publication of this kind requires some measure of financial aid. Having been a beneficiary of the Carnegie Trust for the Universities of Scotland before, I am doubly appreciative of the generous help which I have again received on this occasion.

For permission to reprint material previously published I have to thank the Editors of the following journals: *The Aberdeen University Review*, *German Life and Letters*, *The Modern Language Review*, and *The Publications of the English Goethe Society*.

[1] Publications of the Deutsche Schillergesellschaft, 21; Stuttgart, 1955. Cf. my review in *The Modern Language Review*, LIII, 1, January 1958.

   To Dr. W. Douglas Simpson, our University Librarian, and to his staff I am obliged for their unfailing and ungrudging helpfulness.

   A debt of gratitude of a different order, mounting steadily as the years go by, is acknowledged, *tant bien que mal*, in the dedication.

W. W.

King's College, Aberdeen
   Easter, 1958

CONTENTS

CONTENTS

SCHILLER AND BURNS

I

SCHILLER AND BURNS

ROBERT BURNS and Schiller were born in the same year, and they both died young; Burns in his thirty-eighth year, Schiller at the age of forty-five. In neither case did early death come as a sudden and unforeseeable stroke of fate: it had cast its shadow before, darkening their closing years. Both men, in their different ways, had lived recklessly, burning up their energies, forcing the pace; all too soon their strength was spent, and they were left with no defence against the inroads of disease. When they died, in what should have been the prime of life, both had accomplished enough to leave an immortal memory behind. Burns had sung his song 'for poor auld Scotland's sake' and fulfilled the promise made in his *Epistle to William Simson*:

> We'll gar our streams an' burnies shine
> Up wi' the best!

Schiller had won for himself a place of honour among the world's dramatists, among the great reflective poets, and among the leading theorists of literature. Both poets were busy with new projects when death put an end to their labours. Apart from his contributions to George Thomson's *Select Scottish Airs*, Burns was planning to publish a comprehensive and authorized collection of all the songs of which he wished to be called the author. Schiller's impressive *Demetrius* was half finished. Inevitably, the fame of their achievement is linked with the thought of what might have been, had they been spared longer.

At this point the parallel seems to come to an end: and it does not seem to go very far. The similarities in the external course of the two men's lives do not necessarily argue any inward resemblance, and in themselves they hardly seem to establish any significant analogy. And apart from these biographical correspondences, is there any common ground that would warrant a comparison? At first sight there appears to be very little. The two poets knew nothing of each other, or of each other's works. As Carlyle regretfully remarked, in a letter to Goethe (September 25, 1828): 'It

1

has often struck me to remark that he [Burns] was born a few months only before Schiller, in the year 1759; and that neither of these two men, of whom I reckon Burns perhaps naturally even the greater, ever heard the other's name; but that they shone as stars in opposite hemispheres, the little Atmosphere of the Earth intercepting their mutual light.' Schiller's fame had hardly penetrated into Scotland before Burns's death: Carlyle's *Life of Schiller*, a pioneer work, first appeared (in the *London Magazine*) in 1823–24. Nor did the poems of Burns become at all widely known in Germany during Schiller's lifetime: the early—and, as Carlyle had anticipated, inadequate—translation by Ph. Kaufmann did not appear in print until 1839. Some copies of the Scots originals no doubt circulated in Germany long before that date; but even if Schiller had come across any of these, one may doubt whether he could have made much of them. Even Goethe, whose command of English, acquired at an early stage in his life, was far superior to Schiller's, had to admit that he was often baffled by Burns's idiom. 'Such elements of his poetry as we were able to assimilate', he observes,[1] 'convinced us of his extraordinary talent, and we regretted that the Scots tongue was a hindrance to us precisely at those points where he had no doubt hit upon the purest and most natural expression.' This is not to be wondered at; after all, many Scotsmen born and bred need the help of a glossary for an accurate understanding of such poems as *Halloween* or *The Holy Fair*. How could Schiller, with his sketchy knowledge of English, have appreciated the pliancy and precision of Burns's diction, the sharp bite of his humour, or his superb metrical skill? Conversely, how would Schiller's sustained and deeply serious reflections on the nature and purpose of poetry have struck Burns, had he known about them—Burns, who wrote (in the *Epistle to James Smith*)

> For me, an aim I never fash;
> I rhyme for fun,

and who was inclined to mock at 'the systematic Fathers and Brothers of scientific Criticism'?[2]

Further doubts arise when one considers the stories of the two poets' lives more in detail. Their graphs are similar in shape; but within this general similarity of outline, marked and significant contrasts are noticeable. At the Duke of Suabia's Military Academy, Schiller received, not the training for the ministry which his parents

---

[1] In his introduction to the German edition of Carlyle's *Life of Schiller*.

[2] Letter to the Rev. William Greenfield, December 1786. (No. 66 in J. DeLancey Ferguson's edition of *The Letters of Robert Burns*, Oxford, 1931.)

had had in mind for him and upon which he had set his heart as a boy, but a good general education, followed by a course of professional instruction which made him into a medical practitioner of sorts. He had a competent knowledge of Latin—witness his renderings of lengthy passages from the *Aeneid*—he was well read in contemporary literature and philosophy, and although his lack of conversational fluency in French proved a handicap in his discussions with Mme de Staël, he knew the language well enough to produce, shortly before his death, a remarkably fine translation of *Phèdre*. By comparison, Burns was (as he put it in his *First Commonplace Book*) 'but little indebted to scholastic education'. Not that one ought to think of him as the unlettered ploughman of sentimental tradition; nor was he so exclusively 'Heaven-taught' as Henry Mackenzie suggested in an early review of the Kilmarnock volume. With his eager desire to learn and his power of quick assimilation, he made the most of such opportunities as he was able to snatch when he could be spared from the work of the farm. But how few and how limited were the chances that William Burnes could offer his eldest son: the brief period of elementary schooling at Alloway, the strangely assorted text-books used for study at home, the intermittent visits to the parish school at Dalrymple, the three weeks' stay with his former schoolmaster John Murdoch at Ayr in 1773 (during the last fortnight of which they 'attacked the French with great courage'), and the summer of 1775 at Kirkoswald (so memorably described in the long autobiographical letter to Dr. John Moore), where the 'pretty good progress' he had been making in Mensuration, Surveying, Dialling, etc., came to an abrupt stop when 'the sun entered Virgo', and 'a charming Fillette . . . overset his Trigonometry'. So it continued, 'much in the same tenor', through his later 'teens and early twenties. While Schiller was a full-time student, Robert Burns had to spend by far the greater part of his time and energy helping his father to wrest a living from the ungrateful soil of Mount Oliphant and Lochlie, doing a man's work at the age of fifteen, as the principal labourer on the farm. Nor did this pressure ease except for brief intervals. From start to finish, the story of Burns's life is a story of poverty; such reading as he was able to do (and he contrived to do much more than he is sometimes given credit for)[1] had to be fitted somehow into the hard

<hr />

[1] Cf. his letters to Dr. John Moore, August 2, 1787; to Mrs. Dunlop, May 4, 1788; to Peter Hill, July 18, 1788, and March 2, 1790; to Sir John Sinclair, August or September, 1791. See also James Kinsley's review of Christina Keith, *The Russet Coat*, in the *Modern Language Review*, LII, 3, July 1957.

life of a struggling young farmer. Clearly Schiller had a much better chance of developing his gifts by study and thus adding to his intellectual resources. Not that his life was a bed of roses. After his flight from Stuttgart in 1782 and his failure to establish himself at Mannheim, his plight was unenviable and his prospects bleak. Eight years later, in the early days of his marriage, his financial position as an unsalaried Professor of History in the University of Jena was still far from bright; constant overwork told severely on his health. But even when his funds were at their lowest ebb, his standard of living was markedly superior to what Burns had to be content with, and his hopes for the future higher; he did not see himself lying

> in kilns and barns at e'en,
> When banes are craz'd, and bluid is thin,

as Burns did in his *Epistle to Davie*. What is more important, he contrived to devote himself entirely to his art and to his intellectual pursuits, although at times this meant pocketing his pride, soliciting the patronage of influential men, incurring debts, and accepting charity from various benefactors.

There were moments, it is true, when Schiller thought of securing a steady and adequate income by resuming the study of medicine, taking his doctorate, and establishing himself as a fully qualified physician. When his contract with the Mannheim theatre lapsed in 1784, he went so far as to ask Baron von Dalberg to finance such a scheme by continuing his salary, as an *ex gratia* payment, for another year—the year he would have required to complete his medical qualifications. He tried to add force to his appeal by asserting that this project had long been in his mind: 'For a long time I have been afraid, not without cause, that sooner or later my poetic ardour would die if poetry remained my profession and my livelihood, and that, on the other hand, it was bound to acquire new charm for me as soon as I treated it merely as a recreation, devoting to it only my purest moments.'[1] This argument was meant to convince Dalberg that the money for which Schiller was asking would be well invested: but one may doubt whether the writer was wholly convinced himself. Not that Schiller was deliberately trying to deceive Dalberg; but he was casting about desperately for some way out of his difficulties, and ready to steer for any

[1] In F. Jonas's edition of Schiller's letters, the letter in which this passage occurs is tentatively dated 'end of June (?), 1784'; H. Stubenrauch, however, advances strong arguments in favour of a somewhat later date (first week of September 1784). Cf. his article 'Schiller's Fall—Mannheim, 1784' in *Jahrbuch der deutschen Schillergesellschaft*, I, 1957, pp. 142 ff.

port in the gathering storm—a state of mind in which any man would be apt to deceive himself. When his plea failed, the plan of going back to his 'main line' (Hauptfach), which (as he claimed) 'had long been the only desire of his heart', was soon dismissed: we see him next, not as a physician, but as a journalist, until C. G. Körner's invitation prompted him to shake the dust of Mannheim off his feet. How very different from Burns's philosophical accept-ance of his situation (in the *Epistle to James Smith*)

> The star that rules my luckless lot,
> Has fated me the russet coat. . . .

and from his realistic assessment of his prospects. Even when his 'buble of fame was at the highest', he remained unintoxicated by his success;[1] when he was being lionized, when he was moving among the aristocracy and the intelligentsia of the Capital (with bibulous nights in the company of the Crochallan Fencibles for light relief), when the publication of his *Poems* had restored his finances and provided him with a little ready cash, he had no illusions about his 'late meteorous appearance on the stage of Life',[2] and no thought of becoming what Schiller remained all his life, a professional poet and man of letters. Instead, he negotiated with Patrick Miller for the lease of a farm where he 'might live in humble decency, and have a spare hour now and then to write out an idle rhyme' (January 15, 1787), and wrote to the Earl of Buchan (February 7, 1787): 'I must return to my rustic station, and, in my wonted way woo my rustic Muse at the Plough-tail.' At the same time, knowing from bitter experience the difficulty of making a small, ill-stocked farm pay, he appealed to such patrons as Robert Graham of Fintry and the Earl of Glencairn to recommend him for a position in the Excise, and subsequently took a six weeks' course of instruction to qualify for appointment. Having estab-lished himself in the role of a Scottish Bard by the publication of the Kilmarnock and Edinburgh editions of his *Poems*, he seemed content to treat his contributions to Johnson's *Scots Musical Museum* and to Thomson's *Select Scottish Airs* largely as a labour of love, con-sidering his songs 'either *above*, or *below* price': 'to talk of money, wages, fee, hire, etc. would be downright Sodomy of Soul!'[3]

At Mannheim, at Leipzig, at Weimar and at Jena, Schiller had ready access to libraries; even during the eight months he spent at

---

[1] Letter to the Rev. Wm. Greenfield, December 1786. (No. 66)
[2] Letter to Robert Graham of Fintry, January 1788. (No. 172)
[3] To George Thomson, September 16, 1792.

Bauerbach, his friend Reinwald, the Meiningen librarian, provided him with the books he required. Burns had no such facilities at Mossgiel and at Ellisland, and had to make do with the somewhat limited resources of the Monkland Friendly Society (of which he was treasurer and secretary), eked out by such books as his friend Peter Hill could pick up for him in Edinburgh, 'the cheapest way, the best.' Nor was he much better off at Dumfries; on April 16, 1792, we find him writing to his publisher, W. Creech, who was about to bring out a new edition of his *Poems*: 'A few Books which I very much want, are all the recompence I crave.'

From his early years, Schiller numbered among his acquaintances people of culture and education; at Weimar and Jena, he moved among the intellectual élite of Germany and formed ties of close personal friendship with Goethe and Wilhelm von Humboldt. The only time when Burns enjoyed similar opportunities was during his 'meteorous appearance' in Edinburgh; but his contacts with the Edinburgh intelligentsia were much less close, and much more ephemeral, than Schiller's connexions at Weimar, and the men he met—Professor Dugald Stewart the philosopher, and his predecessor Adam Ferguson; Dr. Hugh Blair; Henry Mackenzie; the ill-starred quondam Moderator the Rev. William Greenfield; kind old Dr. Blacklock; Henry Erskine, Dean of the Faculty of Advocates—were not, on the whole, in the same class as Schiller's friends.

No less marked is the contrast between the domestic lives of the two men. They both married at about the same time of life, Schiller at the age of thirty, Burns at the age of twenty-nine (if the evidence of his correspondence be accepted, and the early months of 1788 taken as the date of his legal marriage, the exact details of which remain obscure).[1] Schiller married Charlotte von Lengefeld, a young lady of good family who appreciated his work and his ambitions, and to whom he remained unswervingly devoted. It is true that the letters written during his courtship, many of which are addressed jointly to his fiancée and to her more brilliant married sister, Caroline von Beulwitz, suggest a certain ambivalence in Schiller's feelings. But though there was potential danger in this courtship *à trois*, the situation is hardly to be compared to the vagaries of Burns's love-life, both before and after his marriage to Jean Armour. The tone of Schiller's life with Charlotte was one

[1] Cf. Maurice Lindsay, *Robert Burns*, London, 1954, pp. 184 f.; Hilton Brown, *There was a Lad*, London, 1949, pp. 215 ff.

of serene contentment, based on mutual affection and respect; it has none of the sordidness which, at times at least, debased Burns's relations with Jean. One cannot conceive of Schiller penning anything like Burns's notorious 'horselitter letter' to Robert Ainslie.[1]

The circumstances of their courtship and their conduct as husbands reflect the two poets' divergent attitudes towards women in general. Schiller in his younger years was decidedly susceptible, and no doubt sowed his wild oats like other young men.[2] There were passing infatuations, such as his flirtation with Lotte von Wolzogen, the daughter of his benefactress, and with Henriette von Arnim at Dresden; there is the doubtful evidence of his Laura poems;[3] and there was his more serious entanglement with Charlotte von Kalb (which, if one looks for a counterpart in Burns's life, might be likened to the Clarinda affair—though it would appear that in spite of moments of 'tender dalliance' when Burns-Sylvander 'seemingly half transgressed the laws of Decorum',[4] Mrs. McLehose kept a tighter rein on her affections than did Frau von Kalb). However, some youthful indiscretions notwithstanding, it remains true that Schiller's fundamental attitude towards women was one of respect, and even of reverence. Among the rich variety of characters in his plays there are some notable villains, but few really wicked women. Of course, his women have their share of common human failings and petty vices: a woman may be coquettish and sensual, like Julia Imperiali in *Fiesco*; stupid and greedy like Frau Miller in *Kabale und Liebe*; weak and vindictive like the Princess Eboli in *Don Carlos*; shrewish, selfish, unforgiving like Queen Isabeau in *Die Jungfrau* (a minor character, and an unconvincing one). But

---

[1] March 3, 1788; No. 215 in J. DeLancey Ferguson's edition of *The Letters of Robert Burns*, Oxford, 1931; vol. I, pp. 199 f.

Maurice Lindsay (loc. cit., pp. 183 f.) speaks of it as 'This quite revoltingly caddish letter, which has drawn more sighs of regret from sentimental Burnsites than anything else the poet committed to paper. . . .' Hilton Brown sounds similarly distressed (loc. cit., p. 223): 'As to the quite dreadful letter to Ainslie—not even a very close or solid friend—one can only wish it not only a lie but a forgery, for it throws the most unbearable light on Burns.' Returning from Edinburgh as a conquering hero, Burns found Jean at Tarbolton, 'banished like a martyr—forlorn, destitute, and friendless; all for the good old cause'. Seeing that Jean was over eight months gone with child, Burns's account of what happened in the course of that reunion certainly makes unedifying reading. But would it really make such a big difference if this letter could be proved 'a lie or a forgery'? After all, there are other letters— to John Arnot (No. 29 in Ferguson's edition), to James Smith (No. 37), to Mrs. McLehose (No. 210)—which show Burns's attitude to 'poor Armour' in a very dubious light.

[2] In his letter to Goethe of December 9, 1794, he speaks of his familiarity with a Bohemian way of life.

[3] Schiller's account of the matter (as reported by Marie Körner) looks harmless enough at first sight, though further reflection may give rise to some doubts. See J. Petersen, *Schillers Gespräche*, Leipzig, 1911, pp. 135 f.

[4] Letter to Mrs. Agnes McLehose, January 25, 1788.

B

only two of his major women characters—Elizabeth in *Maria Stuart*
and Marina in *Demetrius*—have in their nature an irredeemable twist
towards evil. Schiller is enough of a realist to admit the existence
of such women; in his view, however, they are untypical, perver-
sions of the true pattern of womanhood. That essential pattern,
varied according to age, social station, and individual temperament,
may be seen in such characters as Leonore in *Fiesco*, the Queen in
Don Carlos, Thekla in *Wallenstein*, Gertrud Stauffacher in *Tell*; or,
turning to his poetry, in the complementary pictures of girlish
innocence and wifely devotion in *Das Lied von der Glocke*, or again
in the poem *Würde der Frauen*:

> Ehret die Frauen! Sie flechten und weben
> Himmlische Rosen ins irdische Leben,
> Flechten der Liebe beglückendes Band,
> Und in der Grazie züchtigem Schleier
> Nähren sie wachsam das ewige Feuer
> Schöner Gefühle mit heiliger Hand.

To the impertinence of the Schlegels, who sneered at these poems,[1]
Schiller might well have opposed some lines from his poem *Das
Mädchen von Orleans*—lines which refer to Voltaire's *La Pucelle*:

> Krieg führt der Witz auf ewig mit dem Schönen,
> Er glaubt nicht an den Engel und den Gott;
> Dem Herzen will er seine Schätze rauben. . .

The pictures of family life which Schiller draws in *Das Lied von
der Glocke*—of shy and radiant young love, of conjugal affection,
of the practical partnership of husband and wife—are not without
their parallels in Burns: in *The Cottar's Saturday Night* and in *John
Anderson*, that true and touching evocation of an aged couple's
mutual devotion, deepened by a lifetime of loyalty and sweetened
by many shared memories. But much as the reader of Burns may
cherish these poems, he must at the same time admit that the
attitudes which they embody are not wholly characteristic of their
author. The mother in *The Cottar's Saturday Night* may be 'weel-
pleas'd to think her bairn's respected like the lave': but does the
poet himself share the sentiments of the 'blate an' laithfu'' young

---

[1] In a letter to her daughter Auguste Böhmer, dated October 14, 1799, Karoline Schlegel
reported: 'aber über ein Gedicht von Schiller, das *Lied von der Glocke*, sind wir gestern mittag
fast von den Stühlen gefallen vor Lachen . . .' This merriment was partly an expression of
personal animosity, and partly it was prompted by the belief (genuine enough, perhaps,
however mistaken) that Schiller's sentiments were Philistine compared with the Schlegels'
own *avant-garde* views, as set forth in Friedrich Schlegel's *Lucinde*. Thomas Mann has the
appropriate comment: 'Es war doch unangebracht bis zur Schnödigkeit, dies Gelächter der
Ausgepichten gegen das schlechthin Grossartige'. (*Versuch über Schiller*, Berlin and Frankfurt,
1955, p. 13.)

suitor who wins the parents' approval? Is he not rather more like
the rakish seducer, with his 'ensnaring art' and his smooth tongue,
whom he professes to execrate? Had he not in an earlier poem
warned the Mauchline belles against the 'rakish art' of such as himself? Had he not told them to

> Beware a tongue that's smoothly hung,
> A heart that warmly seems to feel

because

> The frank address, and politesse
> Are all finesse in Rob Mossgiel?

It is true that Burns was very conscious of family ties and obligations:

> To make a happy fireside clime
> To weans and wife,
> That's the true pathos and sublime
> Of human life

he declared in the *Epistle to Dr. Blacklock*. It is true, too, that
he took a genuine pride and delight in paternity, legitimate or
otherwise: witness his *Welcome to his Love-Begotten Daughter*, in
which a rebel's defiance and the happy memories of an unrepentant
sensualist—

> Welcome! my bonie, sweet, wee dochter,
> Tho' ye come here a wee unsought for,
> And tho' your comin' I hae fought for,
> Baith kirk and quier;
> Yet, by my faith, ye're no unwrought for,
> That I shall swear!

—blend so charmingly with a father's sense of his new respon-
sibilities. All the same, this note—the note of the paterfamilias—
forms but a modest accompaniment to the *leitmotiv* which sounds
again and again, in poem after exuberant poem: the lure of 'Eve's
bonie squad', of 'dear, deluding woman' who remains 'the joy of
joys' for 'rantin, rovin Robin'. The theme lends itself to modulation
through a variety of keys, reflecting varying moods and attitudes:
the afterglow of gratified desire, as in *The Rigs o' Barley*:

> But a' the pleasures e'er I saw,
> Tho' three times doubl'd fairly—
> That happy night was worth them a',
> Amang the rigs o' barley.
> Corn rigs, an' barley rigs,
> An' corn rigs are bonie:
> I'll ne'er forget that happy night,
> Amang the rigs wi' Annie;

rebellion against moral authority, as in the 'Postscript' to *The Gowden Locks of Anna*:

> The Kirk an' State may join an' tell,
> To do sic things I maunna:
> The Kirk an' State may gae to hell,
> And I'll gae to my Anna;

a naïve pride in his sexual prowess, as in *Nature's Law*:

> Kind Nature's care had given his share
> Large, of the flaming current;
> And, all devout, he never sought
> To stem the sacred torrent—

or in the version of *Green Grow the Rashes* which appears in *The Merry Muses of Caledonia*:

> In sober house I am a priest:
> A hero when I'm tipsy O;
> But I'm a king and every thing,
> When wi' a wanton Gipsey O . . .

or the *insouciant* humour of the 'fornicator by profession'[1] who inevitably thinks of women in the plural

> N'er break your heart for ae rebute,
> But think upon it still, jo:
> That gin the lassie winna do't,
> Ye'll find anither will, jo.—

who has no regrets—

> Their tricks an' craft hae put me daft,
> They've taen me in, an' a' that;
> But clear your decks, an' here's the Sex!
> I like the jads for a' that—

and who remains cheerfully incorrigible:

> A fornicator-lown he call'd me,
> An' said my faut frae bliss expell'd me;
> I own'd the tale was true he tell'd me,

---

[1] This phrase, applied by Burns to himself and his Mauchline friends, occurs in *The Court of Equity*, another piece of Burnsian bawdy in that apocryphal collection, *The Merry Muses of Caledonia*. (For the curious history of that curious collection, see Maurice Lindsay, *Robert Burns*, London, 1954, p. 251, and Cyril Pearl, *Bawdy Burns*, London, 1958, pp. 152 ff.) A collated version of the poem is printed as an Appendix in Catherine Carswell's *Life of Robert Burns*, London, 1930. Extracts from it are quoted by Maurice Lindsay, loc. cit., and by David Daiches, *Robert Burns*, New York, 1950, pp. 314 f.

In a letter to Robert Cleghorn (October 25, 1793[?]) which contains another item from *The Merry Muses*, also with a legal flavour ('Act Sederunt of the Session—A Scots Ballad'), Burns supplies his own vigorous commentary: 'Well! the Law is good for Something, since we can make a B——dy-song out of it.—(N.B.—I never made anything of it in any other way—) There is, there must be, some truth in original sin.—My violent propensity to B——dy convinces me of it.—Lack a day! if that species of Composition be the Sin against "the Haly Ghaist", "I am the most offending soul alive".'

'But, what the matter?
(Quo' I) I fear unless ye geld me,
I'll ne'er be better!'

In this intense and lifelong preoccupation with the physical side of sex, Burns differs radically from Schiller. True, one or two parallels can be found. In the early poem *Männerwürde* (first published under the title *Kastraten und Männer* in the *Anthologie auf das Jahr 1782*) Schiller insists that virility is the prerequisite of creative genius—

> Aus eben diesem Schöpferfluss, (cf. Burns's 'sacred torrent')
> Woraus wir Menschen werden,
> Quillt Götterkraft und Genius,
> Was mächtig ist auf Erden——

and boasts about it (a type of vanity which is, after all, not uncommon among young men); the lines

> Wer keinen Menschen machen kann,
> Der kann auch keinen lieben

might be likened to Burns's

> I'm better pleas'd to make one more,
> Than be the death of twenty.

Thomas Mann notes the same trait in his Essay on Schiller—'a boyishly boastful sensuality, an eroticism which poses as being thoroughly worldly and sophisticated'—and he quotes Fiesco's (designedly frivolous) *mot*: 'Das Frauenzimmer ist nie so schön als im Schlafgewand — es ist die Tracht seines Gewerbes.' It is significant, however, that when, in *Der Venuswagen* (another early piece), Schiller writes on the theme of sexual indulgence, he depicts the Cyprian as a common whore, warns young men against wasting their strength in what Burns calls 'life-giving wars of Venus', and deploys the resources of his medical knowledge in describing the dire penalties of incontinence. All this is clearly poles apart from Burns's lusty, earthy delight in physical passion.

Nor is there anything in Schiller's poetry that can be compared with those of Burns's lyrics in which sexuality is suffused with tenderness: *Mary Morrison, Of a' the Airts, The Banks o' Doon, Blythe hae I been on yon Hill, My Luve is like a red, red Rose, O wert thou in the cauld blast*—to name a few. In these songs Burns is not 'on Parnassus' brink' (as he pictured himself in his *Second Epistle to Davie*), but at the very summit. Songs such as these are outside the compass of Schiller's art, just as Schiller's best and most characteristic poetic achievement is beyond the scope of Burns. Schiller's essential contribution to German poetry lies in his reflective verse, and, to a lesser extent, in some of his ballads. Burns, though endowed with a keen intellect—Carlyle notes the 'vigour of his strictly intellectual perceptions'—is not a thinker.[1] On the other hand, he is, what Schiller is not, a singer. To say this is not to belittle his brilliant verse tales, Epistles, Epitaphs, and Addresses. Indeed, it has been argued that 'if the Songs, his own and those which are effects of a collaboration, be the more national, the Poems are the greater, and it is chiefly to the Poems that Burns is indebted for his place in literature'.[2] Yet for many lovers of Burns, among his fellow-countrymen and elsewhere, his songs remain the crowning glory of his work: songs about the joys and sorrows of country life, about the needs of the senses and the affections of the heart, about man and nature in conflict or in harmony: songs in many of which he re-combines, with breath-taking mastery, elements of traditional Scots folk-songs, giving them unity and finish, blending their ancient life with his own, marrying new words to old tunes. Schiller could never have done anything of the kind, nor did it occur to him to try. He did indeed write, and very perceptively, on the subject of folk poetry, in his essay on Bürger; but he did not produce any. Schiller is, in a sense that remains to be indicated, a popular poet; but he is about as far from being a folk-poet as anyone can be; while Burns has been extolled—and not by Scottish critics only—as 'the folk-poet of the world',[3] 'the one great poet in our language who is also genuinely a popular poet',[4] capable of producing 'a score of masterpieces . . . in which the Vernacular is carried to the highest level it has ever reached in verse'.[5]

In his review of Bürger's poems, Schiller defines the only kind of popularity that he considers worth striving for. Such popularity consists in satisfying the intellectual élite without forfeiting the interest of a wider and less educated public. 'What an undertaking' (he writes)—'to satisfy the fastidious taste of the connoisseur without thereby repelling the masses: to adapt oneself to the childlike minds of the common people without detracting from the dignity of art. The difficulty is great, but not insuperable; the whole secret of its

---

[1] One of his most recent critics states a well-established view when she says that reflection was 'the one quality denied him' (Christina Keith, *The Russet Coat*, London, 1956, p. 174)—though one need not agree with her when she goes on to remark that 'this lack of reflection . . . keeps him, and will always keep him, from the summit of Parnassus. . . .'
[2] W. E. Henley, *Burns*, Edinburgh and London, 1898; pp. 277 f.
[3] A. A. Jack, *Poetry and Prose*, London, 1911, p. 74.
[4] John Drinkwater, *Robert Burns*, Edinburgh, 1924, p. 10.
[5] W. E. Henley, loc. cit., p. 264.

solution lies in a happy choice of subject and extreme simplicity in its treatment.' Schiller condemned Bürger because he had aimed too low. In his own ballads he sought to practise what he had preached, and in most of them he succeeded. Their subjects are arresting and easily grasped, the manner of treatment firm and clear, yet unconstrained. They are a dramatist's ballads: with a few deft touches the exposition is given, the scene is set, the characters are introduced; there is suspense while the action works up to a turning-point, and the dénouement, whether happy or otherwise, comes swiftly and with striking effect. We witness human passions and human conflicts which all readers recognize at once as being timeless and universal. The outlines are bold and clear; there is no chiaroscuro, no baffling ambiguity, nothing eerie—no 'ghosts, fairies, brownies, witches, warlocks, spunkies, kelpies, elf-candles, deadlights, wraiths...'[1] There is, admittedly, a dragon; but the monster in *Der Kampf mit dem Drachen* is a piece of stage machinery, creaking a little at the hinges, quite unlike Wagner's Fafner, for instance, who is part of the mystery and lurking terror of the forest. Schiller's dragon merely serves to set the scene for the real action of the poem, which takes place before the Grand Master and the assembled Knights Hospitallers, and which centres round a moral issue. As so often with Schiller, 'the stage becomes a tribunal' (though it should be noted—a point not always sufficiently appreciated by critics who would write Schiller off as a mere moralizer—that it does not thereby cease to be a stage). What, one wonders, would Schiller have made of *Tam o'Shanter*? When he tells the story of a man who made bold to draw the veil from forbidden mysteries and who by his presumption incurred the wrath of occult powers, he does so in a solemn vein; his poem develops into a gloss on the Fall of Man; the reckless, self-tormenting neophyte of *Das verschleierte Bild zu Sais* has nothing in common with Tam in his ingle nook, 'o'er a' the ills o' life victorious', and it is a far cry from the silent temple of Isis to the witches' sabbath in 'Aloway's auld, haunted kirk'. Again, when Schiller tells a tale of a last-minute escape and rescue—and very effectively he tells it in *Die Bürgschaft*— the creation of suspense, though he manages it with great skill, is not his primary concern. The choice which confronts Damon at the end—

> Zurück! du rettest den Freund nicht mehr,
> So rette das eigene Leben!

is a moral choice; his ordeal culminates in a test of his loyalty;

[1] Cf. Burns's letter to Dr. John Moore, August 2, 1787.

and his resolve to lay down his life on the altar of friendship is an
act of faith which puts the cynical tyrant to shame. What would
Schiller have thought of Burns's treatment of analogous situations in
Tam o' Shanter? Would he have classed it with Bürger's efforts?
Could he have responded to the distinctive appeal of Burns's
poem, even though its excellence is not of the kind he himself aimed
at? He would certainly have discerned its structure with a crafts-
man's eye, noting the variations of *tempo* as the narrative unfolds—
the leisurely opening, the quickening pace as Tam proceeds on his
ride, the *ritardando* effect of the narrator's comments, and the mad
rush at the end. But he could hardly have appreciated Burns's
verbal dexterity, his command of authentic idiom, the ingenuity and
unerring rightness of phrasing and rhyme. And would he have
relished the sheer exuberance of the poem, its bursting vitality, its
mixture of Breughel-like realism and grotesque fantasy? And
finally, would he have approved of the irony of the narrator's
moralizing comments which, while purporting to censure Tam
and to present his adventure as a cautionary tale, are in fact designed
to engage our sympathies ever more securely on the side of the
'bletherin, blusterin, drunken blellum'? (The irony is the more
elusive as the narrator, who repeatedly speaks in the first person—
'Ah, gentle dames! it gars me greet . . .'; 'But to our tale . . .'—is not
identical with the author: he is a *persona* whom the poet interposes
between himself and his audience.[1] In short, would Schiller have
appreciated the humour of the poem?

There are those, even among his admirers, who profess to find
no trace of humour in Schiller's make-up. Carlyle speaks of his
'singular want' of it, and goes on to say: 'Among all writers of
any real poetic genius, we cannot recollect one who, in this respect,
exhibits such total deficiency as Schiller. In his whole writings
there is scarcely any vestige of it, scarcely any attempt that way.
His nature was without Humour.' Carlyle's judgment, as usual, is
admirably clear-cut: but is it correct? Do some of Schiller's letters

---

[1] In his stimulating article 'Wer erzählt den Roman?' (*Deutschunterricht für Ausländer*,
VII, 6, November-December 1957, pp. 161 ff.), Wolfgang Kayser points out 'dass der Er-
zähler in aller Erzählkunst niemals der bekannte oder noch unbekannte Autor ist, sondern eine
Rolle, die der Autor erfindet und einnimmt', and he goes on to speak of 'die auffällige Leich-
tigkeit, mit der ein Ich-Erzähler sich zwischen seinem (undeutlichen) Erzählerstandpunkt und
dem Erzählten hin und her bewegt'. Several passages in *Tam o'Shanter* show this double perspective. Take these lines, for example:

> Now, do thy speedy utmost, Meg,
> And win the key-stane o' the brig;

is this the narrator commenting on the events of his tale, or is it a cry from the very heart
of the narrative at its climax?

not afford evidence of a sense of humour—his chronicle of events at Bauerbach and Mannheim, for example,[1] his early impressions of Weimar and Jena, his deft thumb-nail sketches of new acquaintances, his entertaining comments on Mme de Staël's visit to Weimar?[2] Does a book like Julius Petersen's *Schillers Gespräche* reflect an entirely humourless personality? Is there not a touch of humour in such poems as *Pegasus im Joche* and *Die Teilung der Erde*? (The more deliberately facetious efforts of his early period—*Bacchus im Triller, Die Rache der Musen, Bauernständchen, Wunderseltsame Historia, Bittschrift*—are in poor taste, and the less said about them the better.) And what of such characters as Spiegelberg in *Die Räuber*, the Moor in *Fiesco* (a comic figure of considerable vitality), or Isolani in *Wallenstein*?

Carlyle's sweeping indictment stands in need of qualification; but though he spoils his case by overstating it, it must be conceded that he has a case. Schiller is not devoid of humour; but with him humour is not, as it is with Burns, a determining feature in the cast of his mind, a pervasive and permanent mode of feeling: it is accidental rather than essential. Without the humorous elements in his work, Schiller would be the poorer, though still recognizably himself: Burns without his humour would not be Burns. The difference goes deep; but in one sphere at least—the sphere of satire—the two poets would have found common ground. Schiller's satirical gift was revealed at an early stage in his caricature of a foppish, brainless, and worthless courtier in *Kabale und Liebe*; it appeared again, more subdued this time, in his portrayal of a crafty, scheming priest in *Don Carlos*; aided and abetted by Goethe, he put it to further use in his *Xenien* and *Votivtafeln*. As a fellow-practitioner, he would have appreciated Burn's accomplished technique as a satirist; what is more, the feelings of resentment and indignation that prompted some of Burns's best satirical poems would have struck an answering chord in Schiller's heart.

Both men abominated hypocrisy and censorious self-righteousness in matters of morals and religion. The 'unco guid' whom Burns pilloried so unforgettably—

> O ye wha are sae guid yoursel,
> Sae pious and sae holy,
> Ye've nought to do but mark and tell
> Your neibours' fauts and folly!

are, of course, a universal type, and it is not surprising that their

---

[1] Cf. his letters to Henriette von Wolzogen, April 23, May 8, and November 13–14, 1783.
[2] Letters to Goethe, December 21, 1803; January 13 and February 16, 1804.

German cousins should figure among the exhibits in Schiller's chamber of horrors, as they do in two *Tabulae Votivae*—*Moralische Schwätzer*:

> Wie sie mit ihrer reinen Moral uns, die Schmutzigen, quälen!
> Freilich, der groben Natur dürfen sie gar nichts vertraun!

and *Meine Antipathie*:

> Herzlich ist mir das Laster zuwider, und doppelt zuwider
> Ist mirs, weil es so viel schwatzen von Tugend gemacht.

The general theme is the same, though there are obvious differences in treatment and emphasis. Burns turns the shafts of his satire against those who, shielded by their own unblemished reputation, presume to cast stones at 'poor Frailty'; Schiller (whose private life did not invite censure and who had no need to defend himself on that score) is more concerned with the moralists' unwelcome intrusion into the aesthetic sphere. What he resents particularly is the practice of literary 'Holy Willies' who contrive to make the best of both worlds, striking moral attitudes and at the same time boosting their sales by a judicious admixture of near-pornography:

> Wollt ihr zugleich den Kindern der Welt und den Frommen gefallen?
> Malet die Wollust, nur—malet den Teufel dazu!

In the evolution of their religious beliefs and doubts, and in their attitude towards organized religion, the two men show a distinct affinity. Both were reared in a home atmosphere of sincere if somewhat narrow Protestant piety. Their childhood was dominated, for better and for worse, by the precept and example of the head of the family. The father figure is one of the archetypes of Schiller's drama, and the father-son conflict is one of his most fruitful themes. The 'priest-like father' in *The Cottar's Saturday Night* who 'reads the sacred page' and 'mixes a' wi' admonition due' is modelled on William Burnes. Schiller's father was more comfortably placed and better educated than Burns's, but fundamentally the two men were very much alike: in their assertion of parental authority, in their fervent belief in education, in their conscious rectitude, in their deep-rooted distrust of their sons' artistic temperament, in their austere and somewhat moralizing piety, as well as in the stress they laid, in home life and family worship, on the lessons that may be learnt from Scripture. For Burns, as for many under-privileged people of his day, the Bible, with its unique blend of history, revelation, prophecy, and poetry, was the main basis of his

early education, and the role which it played in the formation of
Schiller's mind is hardly less important: witness the free use of
scriptural allusions and the echoes of scriptural phrases in the writings
of both poets.

Such an upbringing does not guarantee easy religious conformity
in later life. One claim, however, may fairly be made for it: it
presents religion to the child's mind as a crucial issue that cannot be
ignored—something to be accepted or rejected, but not to be by-
passed. Both Burns and Schiller assimilated and retained certain
elements of the religious instruction they had received at home:
their belief in the existence of God (held, it is true, in a much more
deistic sense than their fathers would have approved of), their respect
for the person of Jesus, and their special regard for the Bible, if
not as the outcome of plenary inspiration, at least as an incomparable
record of religious experience. But they were selective in their
acceptance, and there was much that they felt compelled to reject.
Neither of them was insensitive to the spirit of the gospel—

> Religion des Kreuzes, nur du verknüpftest, in *einem*
> Kranze, der Demut und Kraft doppelte Palme zugleich

Schiller wrote in *Die Johanniter*—but they both felt that that spirit
was not alive in the churches of their day; that their dogmas were
ill-founded, their liturgies empty and arbitrary conventions, their
clergy usurpers of spiritual authority; that they worshipped in vain,
teaching for doctrines the commandments of men.

> The Power, incens'd, the pageant will desert,
> The pompous strain, the sacerdotal stole.

The stimulus of the Reformation—'the revolt against Church
statutes and the return to the sources: the Bible and Reason', as
Schiller put it[1]—was short-lived; as soon as the revolutionary
ferment had settled, there emerged the new orthodoxies of Lutherans
and Calvinists. Since these orthodoxies did not command Burns's and
Schiller's assent, and since outward compliance without inner conviction was repugnant to their nature, they remained outside the fold.[2]

---

[1] Letter to Goethe, September 17, 1800.

[2] There are passages in Burns's and in Schiller's correspondence which would seem to
support a different view; but it is doubtful—to say the least—whether such passages can be
taken at their face value. For instance, in a letter to his elderly friend Mrs. Dunlop (August 22,
1792), Burns, after admitting that 'the damned dogmas of reasoning Philosophy throw in
their doubts' about the possibility of a life beyond the grave, writes as follows: 'However,
I am so convinced that an unshaken faith in the doctrines of Christianity is not only necessary
by making us better men, but also by making us happier men, that I shall take every care
that your little godson, & every little creature that shall call me, Father, shall be firmly

> But twenty times I rather would be
> An atheist clean,
> Than under gospel colours hid be
> Just for a screen

wrote Burns in his *Epistle to the Rev. John M' Math*, one of the 'candid liberal band' of New-Light ministers at whose tables (as Carlyle rather strangely puts it) Burns 'learned much more than was needful for him'. Schiller similarly defines his position in the distich *Mein Glaube*:

> Welche Religion ich bekenne? Keine von allen,
> Die du mir nennst! — Und warum keine? — Aus Religion.

A man who in those days rejected the doctrines of the Church could hardly be expected to take kindly to its discipline. Burns, the 'fornicator-lown', was bound to run foul of the ministers and elders who, through the Kirk Session, supervised the conduct of their parishioners in eighteenth-century Scotland. Small wonder that Burns's revolt against the established Church was more violent than Schiller's. The unruly Bard resented the attentions of 'the holy beagles, the houghmagandie pack',[1] and he took a humorist's revenge, bestowing a most unenviable kind of immortality on his self-righteous contemporaries with

> Their sighin', cantin', grace-proud faces,
> Their three-mile prayers, an' half-mile graces,
> Their raxin conscience,

satirizing the antics of their preachers in *The Twa Herds* and *The Holy Fair*, and questioning the sincerity of their faith

> When men display to congregations wide
> Devotion's ev'ry grace, except the heart!

Schiller, however, could hit equally hard on occasion; for instance, in the last two lines of the quatrain *An die Frommen*:

> Herzlos ist eure Andacht kaltes Fieber,
> Kopflos ist nur ein Popanz euer Gott.

There is a passage in *Der Geisterseher*, near the beginning of Book 2,

---

persuaded that "God was in Christ, reconciling the world unto himself, not imputing unto men their trespasses".'

Two comments may be suggested. Firstly, Burns does not say that he is convinced of the truth of the doctrines in question; he merely says that it is a good thing to believe in them because such faith makes people better and happier. (In a later epistle to Mrs. Dunlop— the relevant section is dated New Year's Day, 1795—he states that he has 'nothing to say to any body, as, to which Sect they belong, or what Creed they believe.') Secondly, he is trying to give pleasure to this particular correspondent by speaking her language.

Something similar might be said about analogous passages in some of Schiller's letters to his parents and to Frau von Wolzogen.

[1] Letter to John Arnot; No. 29 in DeLancey Ferguson's edition.

which shows how well Schiller understood the effects of a repressive
religious upbringing. Throughout his boyhood and adolescence,
religion appears to the hero not as a blessing, but as an enemy of all
natural impulses and a scourge of the passions, and his sense of
frustration gradually deepens into smouldering resentment:

> Allen seinen kindischen und jugendlichen Neigungen, denen ein derber Körper
> und eine blühende Gesundheit um so kraftvollere Explosionen gab, stand die
> Religion im Wege; mit allem, woran sein jugendliches Herz sich hängte, lag sie
> im Streite; er lernte sie nie als eine Wohltat, nur als eine Geissel seiner Leiden-
> schaften kennen. So entbrannte allmählich ein stiller Groll gegen sie in seinem
> Herzen . . .

The passage might have been written with Burns in mind.

Schiller's and Burns's anti-clericalism, their refusal to conform
in outward observance where they could not believe in their
hearts, was an expression of their faith in intellectual freedom. As
Goethe pointed out to Eckermann (January 18, 1827), the idea of
freedom runs through the whole of Schiller's *œuvre*: to call Schiller
'the poet of freedom' is to use one of the established clichés of
German literary criticism. The phrase fits Burns equally well.
Both men abhorred tyranny in all its forms, religious, social, and
political. In Schiller's thinking, the idea of freedom developed,
acquiring new and more subtle connotations, as he matured.
Burns had less time to mature: 'properly speaking' (as Carlyle
reminds us), 'there is but one era in the life of Burns, and that the
earliest'. However, with Burns as with Schiller the meaning of
freedom has many variants. The word may signify something
wholly negative—the outright rejection of all law and order and
social convention—as it does on the lips of the robbers in Schiller's
first play when they sing:

> Ein freies Leben führen wir,
> Ein Leben voller Wonne.

Whatever their leader's scruples and finer feelings, these are mere
anarchist outlaws, like the Jolly Beggars in Burns's Cantata, whose
prototypes the poet had met at Poosie Nansie's inn at Mauchline.
The veteran soldier and his doxy, the fiddler, and the tinker may be
less criminal characters than Schiller's highwaymen, but their
anarchist creed is the same:

> A fig for those by law protected!
> Liberty's a glorious feast!
> Courts for cowards were erected,
> Churches built to please the priest.

A plea for freedom may take the form of a protest against class barriers and against privilege of birth or wealth unsupported by merit, as in Schiller's *Kabale und Liebe* and in Burns's *Epistle to Dr. Blacklock*—

> But why should ae man better fare,
> And a' men brithers?—

in *A Man's a Man for a' that*—

> Ye see yon birkie ca'd 'a lord',
> Wha struts, an' stares, an' a' that;
> Tho' hundreds worship at his word,
> He's but a coof for a' that;—

in *The Twa Dogs* or in the *Epistle to Davie*:

> It's hardly in a body's pow'r,
> To keep, at times, frae being sour,
> To see how things are shar'd;
> How best o' chiels are whyles in want,
> While coofs on countless thousands rant,
> And ken na how to ware't.

The natural corollary of such protests is the affirmation that men, as men, are all equal, whatever their social status may be:

> The rank is but the guinea's stamp,
> The Man's the gowd for a' that—

or as Schiller puts it in *An die Freude*:

> Männerstolz vor Königsthronen—
> Brüder, gält es Gut und Blut:
> Dem Verdienste seine Kronen,
> Untergang der Lügenbrut!

Such sentiments recall the catchwords of the French Revolution, and indeed it would have been surprising if Burns and Schiller had not at first felt some measure of sympathy with the revolutionary movement. They were attuned to its Rousseauist ideology. On the other hand, they were not prepared to condone, let alone approve, the brutality of its demagogues and the ugly excesses of mob rule. The French National Assembly might confer honorary citizenship on the author of *Die Räuber*, but even if the diploma had reached him sooner than it did, 'M. Gille' would not have wanted any truck with 'those beastly butchers'.[1] Burns might think Louis XVI a 'perjured Blockhead' and Marie Antoinette an 'unprincipled Prostitute',[2] and he might flaunt his views on French

---

[1] Cf. his letter to G. Körner, February 8, 1793. Schiller's attitude towards the French Revolution is discussed more fully in the essay on 'Law and the Social Order in Schiller's Thought': *vide infra*.

[2] Cf. his letter to Mrs. Dunlop, January 12, 1795.

politics with his customary panache; but when he was 'accused to the Board of Excise of being a Republican' and 'a person disaffected to Government', he lost no time in defining the nature of his 'Reform opinions' and in affirming that he held 'the British Constitution, as settled at the Revolution, to be the most glorious Constitution on earth, or that perhaps the wit of man can frame'. It is true that the letters in which he did so[1] were intended to clear his character as a civil servant at a time when he was in fear of losing his job; however, there is no need to assume that, being an apologia, they must be wholly untrustworthy. Contemplating the dangers, on the one hand, of autocratic misrule, and, on the other, of mob violence, Burns felt inclined to say 'A plague o' both your houses!':

> The wretch that would a *tyrant* own,
> And the wretch, his true-born brother,
> Who would set the *Mob* aboon the *Throne*,
> May they be damn'd together!——

or, more tersely still (in the *Lines on the Commemoration of Rodney's Victory*):

> Be ANARCHY curs'd, and be TYRANNY damn'd!

Schiller, too, had damned tyranny with great zest in his day; but the spectacle of Girondin vainglory and Jacobin terror did not inspire much confidence in the healthy instincts of the masses or in the political sagacity of their spokesmen:

> Freiheit ruft die Vernunft, Freiheit die wilde Begierde,
> Von der heilgen Natur ringen sie lüstern sich los.
> Ach, da reissen im Sturm die Anker, die an dem Ufer
> Warnend ihn hielten, ihn fasst mächtig der flutende Strom,
> Ins Unendliche reisst et ihn hin, die Küste verschwindet,
> Hoch auf der Fluten Gebirg wiegt sich entmastet der Kahn;
> Hinter Wolken erlöschen des Wagens beharrliche Sterne,
> Bleibend ist nichts mehr, es irrt selbst in dem Busen der Gott.

When the militant, annexationist character of revolutionary France became apparent, when in the autumn of 1792 the self-styled champions of liberty began to 'liberate' neighbouring states, many people who had been, like Burns, 'enthusiastic votaries in the beginning of the business',[2] changed their minds. Under threat of foreign invasion, the idea of freedom came to be increasingly identified, in Britain as in Germany, with national independence. That patriotic

---

[1] To Robert Graham of Fintry, December 31, 1792 and January 5, 1793; to John F. Erskine, April 13, 1793.
[2] Cf. his letter to Robert Graham, January 5, 1793.

note sounds as plainly in 'Scots, wha hae wi' Wallace bled' and 'Does haughty Gaul invasion threat?' as it does, later, in *Wilhelm Tell*:

> Unser ist durch tausendjährigen Besitz
> Der Boden — und der fremde Herrenknecht
> Soll kommen dürfen und uns Ketten schmieden
> Und Schmach antun auf unsrer eignen Erde?

Transcending all these various conceptions of freedom there is another: the inward freedom of the soul which is independent of outward circumstances. This idea occupies a place of special importance in Schiller's thought. A man who is master of himself, and at the same time at peace with himself, can pit the strength of his spirit against the worst that life may have in store for him and emerge from the ordeal, shattered and broken, perhaps, yet—paradoxically—triumphant even in defeat. This is the freedom of the hero, the martyr, the saint: a state of mind not easily attained. Even so, the undeniable fact that it has been attained by some shows that it is the birthright of all men:

> Den Mensch ist frei geschaffen, ist frei,
> Und würd er in Ketten geboren;

and while most people may never win through to it in their daily lives, they can partake of it, momentarily and vicariously, through the medium of poetry and drama, through music and art.

This conception of freedom derives from Schiller's encounter with Kant's philosophy and reflects the austerity of Kant's doctrine.[1] No doubt it would be unreasonable to look for any close analogy in Burns; but do we not catch a faintly echoing note once or twice? —in the *Epistle to Davie*, for example:

> And, even should misfortunes come,
> I, here wha sit, hae met wi' some—
>   An's thankfu' for them yet.
> They gie the wit of age to youth;
>   They let us ken oursel;
> They make us see the naked truth—
>   The real guid and ill:

---

[1] Cf. *Kritik der praktischen Vernunft*, Part I, Book i, Secton 3 (Von den Triebfedern der reinen praktischen Vernunft):
  'Es (i.e. the origin of Duty) kann nichts Minderes sein, als was den Menschen über sich selbst (als einen Teil der Sinnenwelt) erhebt, was ihn an eine Ordnung der Dinge knüpft, die nur der Verstand denken kann, und die zugleich die ganze Sinnenwelt, mit ihr das empirisch bestimmbare Dasein des Menschen in der Zeit . . . unter sich hat. Es ist nichts anders als die *Persönlichkeit*, d.i. die Freiheit und Unabhängigkeit von dem Mechanismus der ganzen Natur . . .'

or in the *Epistle to a young Friend*:

> The fear o' hell's a hangman's whip,
>   To haud the wretch in order;
> But where ye feel your honour grip,
>   Let that ay be your border:
> Its slightest touches, instant pause—
>   Debar a' side-pretences;
> And resolutely keep its laws,
>   Uncaring consequences.

For a moment the humorous, conversational tone of these poems changes; a note of pathos is sounded, reminiscent of the pathos that inhabits the world of Schiller's poems and plays. It is no more than a fleeting suggestion, and the resemblance, such as it is, does not obscure the differences. Schiller sees the crises of life—be they caused by hostile circumstance or by a heart divided against itself—as a battleground where man defends his integrity; or, to phrase it in language of a different kind (language that often suggests itself where Schiller is concerned, despite his unorthodoxy), where man fights to save his soul, if need be at the price of all that he holds dear. These are the solemn 'moments of truth' when man stands, awestruck, on the brink of eternity:

> Wo an der Ewigkeit Meer schaudernd der Sterbliche steht.

Such sustained solemnity did not come natural to Burns; when he deliberately attempted it, the results were unimpressive, as in *Tragic Fragment* and *Remorse*—fragments both of them, and not particularly good ones. He preferred to shrug off misfortune with a defiant quip:

> Fortune! if thou'll but gie me still
> Hale breeks, a scone, an' whisky gill,
> An' rowth o' rhyme to rave at will,
>   Tak a' the rest . . . .;

as for moral conflicts, his favourite way to get rid of temptation was to yield to it—not cynically, nor without a sense of guilt, but with a disarmingly cheerful avowal of his own weakness:

> And others, like your humble servan',
> Poor wights! nae rules nor roads observin,
> To right or left eternal swervin,
>   They zig-zag on.

Burns's humour was the solvent which removed the bitterness of moral conflict and kept him in favour with himself. To attain, in the normal conduct of life, the ideal of a balanced personality, as Schiller conceived it in *Über Anmut und Würde* and elsewhere, a

C

man must so condition the impulses of unregenerate nature as to
keep them in tune with the dictates of his conscience: duty must
lose its compulsive, Kantian character and become second nature.
In the years of his maturity, Schiller went a long way towards
achieving this balance in himself. Burns never approached, and
probably never envisaged, such a state of moral grace. And yet, in
his own way his personality had the same kind of wholeness, of
self-sufficiency, of innate authority, that distinguished Schiller's.
The reminiscences of Goethe and of Sir Walter Scott bear striking
witness to this. Commenting on a record of Schiller's conversations
with Christine von Wurmb, Goethe remarked (September 11,
1828):

> Schiller erscheint hier, wie immer, im absoluten Besitz seiner erhabenen Natur;
> er ist so gross am Theetisch, wie er es im Staatsrath gewesen seyn würde. Nichts
> geniert ihn, nichts engt ihn ein, nichts zieht den Flug seiner Gedanken herab; was
> in ihm von grossen Ansichten lebt, geht immer frey heraus ohne Rücksicht und
> ohne Bedenken. Das war ein rechter Mensch, und so sollte man auch seyn!

And Scott, recalling what struck him most forcibly when, as a lad
of fifteen, he met Burns at Professor Ferguson's house, describes the
poet thus:

> His conversation expressed perfect self-confidence, without the slightest
> presumption. Among the men who were the most learned of their time and
> country, he expressed himself with perfect firmness, but without the least intrusive
> forwardness. . . . I do not speak *in malam partem*, when I say, I never saw a man
> in company with his superiors in station or information more perfectly free from
> either the reality or the affectation of embarrassment.

The same common factor—the unaffected[1] self-expression of a
many-sided yet well-integrated personality—can be seen in their
letters. Again the contrasts are self-evident. Burns's letters are much
the more entertaining, Schiller's are intellectually more satisfying.
Burns is more *dégagé*, and correspondingly more formless; Schiller's
letters are more deliberately composed and more heavily burdened
with reflection. To the end of his life Burns let himself go in a
jovial, bantering hail-fellow-well-met manner which Schiller—
in so far as he adopted it at all[2]—abandoned very soon. Schiller's
collected letters, like Burns's, form an illuminating autobiography,
but the accents are placed differently. The autobiography which

---

[1] Like Schiller in his early letters to Baron von Dalberg, Burns becomes affected when he
wants to be ceremonious, in letters to such patrons and socially superior acquaintances as the
Earl of Buchan (though in this case, the stilted diction was sometimes used with deliberate
irony, as in the letter of August 29, 1791), Robert Graham of Fintry (sometimes), the Rev.
John Geddes, or Lady Winifred Maxwell Constable. But these exercises in the formal
epistolary convention of the eighteenth century are the exceptions.

[2] His letter to F. W. von Hoven of February 4, 1781, is an example.

emerges from Schiller's letters[1] is primarily a spiritual one. Not that the little details of everyday life are lacking—a request for half a pound of snuff, a bottle of Burgundy to mark an occasion, a fowl for dinner, bouts of fever, the price of firewood and laundry, the weather, scraps of gossip, the children's measles, a game of cards: it is all there, but it is subordinate to the main theme—the growth of the writer's mind, his development as a poet and a thinker. In Burns's letters, the little things seem to matter more; they are interesting in their own right. A present of cheese (' 'tis but a very little one') for cousin James; the poet's Edinburgh landlady, 'a piously-disposed, sculdudery-abhoring Widow, coming on her grand climacterick . . . at present in sore tribulation respecting some "Daughters of Belial" who are on the floor immediately above'; 'twa wee sarkies', a gift from Clarinda to Sylvander's little son; the broaching of a cask of whisky which 'will bear five waters, strong; or six, ordinary Toddy'; requests for books, including on one occasion a family Bible for a country neighbour, 'the larger the better, but second-handed, for he does not chuse to give above ten shillings'; an application to the Lord Provost, Bailies, and Town Council of Dumfries for remission of school fees; the poet-exciseman 'stormstead', and very drunk, at the 'wicked little village' of Ecclefechan—passages such as these, and many others like them, reflect, in their unstudied prose, that firm hold on the concrete fact, that flair for the flavour of a particular incident, that sense of lived experience which distinguish Burns's verse at its incomparable best.

Any comparison of Burns's and Schiller's letters must allow for the character and the calibre of the recipients. Apart from Goethe, the list of Schiller's principal correspondents includes Christian Gottfried Körner, Wilhelm von Humboldt, Johann Friedrich Cotta: men of taste and considerable distinction, by whose opinions Schiller set much store. Is there, on the other hand, a single one among Burns's correspondents who could meet him on level terms? Schiller moved habitually among men of real intellectual stature; above all, he enjoyed the privilege of friendship and literary partnership with the greatest poet of his age. After having read the Goethe-Schiller correspondence which had just been published, Carlyle remarked, in a letter to Goethe (October 23, 1830):

How different was his fate from that of our own poor Burns, blest with an equal talent, as high a spirit; but smitten with a far heavier curse, and to whom no

[1] Cf. W. Witte, *Schiller*, Oxford, 1949, Part I, ch. 1: Autobiography in Letters.

guiding Friend, warmly as his heart could love, and still long for wisdom, was ever given! One such as you might have saved him, and nothing else could. . . . He was of Schiller's age; in the second year of that fair Weimar union, Burns perished miserably, deserted and disgraced, in that same Dumfries, where they have erected Mausoleums over him, now that it is all unavailing. . . .

It was surely not altogether fortuitous that Schiller and Burns should have been thus linked in Carlyle's mind. Nor was it merely because Carlyle was the only Scotsman of his day and age who had made a really profound study of contemporary German literature; nor, again, was it merely because the two poets happened to be born in the same year. Enough has been said, perhaps, to show that these coincidences are not, in fact, the only basis of comparison. Although the two poets 'shone as stars in opposite hemispheres', something is to be gained by relating their orbits; and it may be added, in conclusion, that further support for this view is to be found in the nature of their posthumous fame and popularity. Both Burns and Schiller have come to be thought of as being, in a special sense, national poets. In the case of Burns the reasons are plain. He has no rival among the poets of his native land, and the 'Scotish pre-judice' which the story of Wallace had poured into his veins at an early age[1] is evident everywhere in his work. Schiller's case is less simple. He does not occupy the same position of unchallenged pre-eminence among the poets of his country; nor does he wear his patriotism with the same kind of air. Other German poets—Eichendorff, Hölderlin, and even the ever-ambiguous Heine—have written more lovingly, more poignantly, of Germany as their home and their mother, and of the secrets of her soul. And yet, at times when national feeling runs high, and people are casting about for someone who will put their thoughts into words for them, it is Schiller to whom they will most readily turn.[2]

Curiously enough, the high regard in which Schiller and Burns are held by the broad masses of their fellow-countrymen is based, at least in part, on misconceptions. Schiller has been idolized for the wrong reasons; passages from his poems and plays, torn from their context, have had to serve as texts for all sorts of political propaganda, and there was a time when an adulterated, syrupy version of his 'idealism' provided a comforting substitute for the Sunday sermon in an increasingly secular civilization. His exacting gospel

[1] Letter to Dr. John Moore, August 2, 1787.

[2] In one of his conversations with Eckermann (January 4, 1824), Goethe noted an analogous paradox: 'Schiller', he remarked, 'who—between ourselves—was much more of an aristocrat than myself, but who was more guarded in his utterances than I was, had the remarkable good fortune of passing for a special friend of the people'.

of the aesthetic education of man did not convert the multitude; it was proclaimed by a voice that cried in the wilderness. As for Burns, those who study him seriously soon discover that the evidence of his poetry and prose does not support the one-sided notions which many of his fellow-countrymen have formed of the national Bard—notions ranging (to quote the Editor of his letters) from 'the sugar-coated poet of the Birthday orators' to 'the profligate of the smoke-room anecdotes'.[1]

These popular fallacies are apt to darken counsel. However, underlying the welter of uninformed opinion there are some plain facts. Though both poets have had more than their fair share of uncritical praise, as well as unjust censure, their popular appeal, undiminished after a century and a half, is clearly genuine. Obscured but not invalidated by all the false assumptions, there is a true response from the man in the street: a response to the work of two poets who both knew, in their different ways, how to give pithy and memorable form to thoughts and feelings familiar to all, in language simple enough to convey something to the meanest intelligence, and at the same time so felicitous as to make perfection look easy. It is a rare gift (not to be confused, as Thomas Mann reminds us in his Essay on Schiller,[2] with that cunning but impure blend of childlike naïveté and hyper-sophistication which is the mark of decadence), and Schiller and Burns both possessed it in an exceptional degree. They use it each in his own distinctive way; Burns is more humorous, more homely, more racy, Schiller more dignified and more resounding. It is the difference between

> The best-laid schemes o' mice an' men
> Gang aft agley

and

> Doch mit des Geschickes Mächten
> Ist kein ewger Bund zu flechten,
> Und das Unglück schreitet schnell . . .

or between

> Wha will be a traitor knave?
> Wha can fill a coward's grave?
> Wha' sae base as be a slave?

and

> Nichtswürdig ist die Nation, die nicht
> Ihr Alles freudig setzt an ihre Ehre—

but it is the same gift. 'What oft was thought, but ne'er so well

---

[1] DeLancey Ferguson, *Selected Letters of Robert Burns*, The World's Classics, 1953, p. xi.
[2] *Versuch über Schiller*, Berlin and Frankfurt, 1955, p. 66.

expressed' acquires, by virtue of the expression and of the personality that informs it, the finality and permanence of art. Schiller and Burns are both eminently quotable; not a few quotations from their works have passed into everyday speech, and they have stood up remarkably well to the merciless wear and tear of common usage. And just as some of their lines and phrases have entered into the very texture of their two languages—how often people use them without being aware of their authorship!—so their personalities and their works are woven into the fabric of their countries' heritage, part of the living past from which the present draws its sustenance. Successive generations of their compatriots may have had mistaken ideas about them: but they have shown a sound instinct in taking them to their hearts.

II

SCOTTISH INFLUENCE ON SCHILLER

THE great flowering of Scottish letters in the eighteenth century
was observed with keen interest on the Continent, and not least
in Germany, where the Scottish philosophers as well as the Scottish
poets and historians found many appreciative readers. One of these
was Schiller. Scottish influence is clearly discernible in his writings,
especially—though not exclusively—in the earlier period of his life
which preceded his study of Kant. Indeed, it may be argued that
in him that influence appears particularly pervasive, for it has left
its mark on each of the three main branches of his work—on his
poetry and drama, on his historical studies, and on his philosophical
reflections.

As one would expect, Schiller's indebtedness to contemporary
Scottish literature and thought has been duly noted by most of his
biographers. (Strangely enough, Carlyle, whose *Life of Schiller*
was one of the first in the field, contents himself with a brief and
none too flattering comment on the 'common-sense philosophy of
the Scotch'—'a poor philosophy, perhaps, but not so poor as none
at all'—and a passing reference to Robert Watson's *History of
Philip II*.) Even in the larger biographies, however, the treatment
accorded to the subject is usually rather piecemeal, to suit the chronological sequence of the narrative. It is the purpose of this brief essay
to offer a connected account.

Schiller never visited Scotland. In fact, he never travelled beyond
the frontiers of Germany: even the local colour in *Wilhelm Tell*, so
admirably vivid and convincing, was produced without any first-
hand knowledge of the Swiss scene. His command of English was,
on his own admission, very inadequate; and apart from a brief and
rather non-committal reference to some Scots visitors in a letter to
Goethe (December 25, 1796), his correspondence reveals no direct
personal contacts with Scots people. (It would be a trifle fanciful to
regard his acquaintance with Frau von Schardt—a lady who, on her
father's side, was descended from the Irvines of Drum—as a link
with Aberdeenshire.[1]) Thus it was not because of any obvious

[1] Concordia Elisabet von Schardt was the mother of Charlotte von Stein. Frau von
Schardt's Scots ancestor was one Gilbert Irwing, who emigrated from Aberdeen to Prussia
in the fifteenth century and served in the army of the Teutonic Knights. Cf. Lt.-Col.
Jonathan Forbes Leslie, *The Irvines of Drum and Collateral Branches*, Aberdeen, 1909, pp. 190 f.

29

predisposing factor that Schiller came under Scottish influence—
a striking testimony to the vitality and the potent appeal of Scottish
literary culture at that time.

Of all the books of Scottish provenance that reached Germany in
the second half of the eighteenth century, none scored a greater or a
more immediate popular success than James Macpherson's *Ossian.*
It is now fairly generally agreed that the Ossianic poems are a product
of the poetic imagination in a different and a more specific sense
than their 'translator' chose to admit. But when they first appeared,
many enthusiastic readers accepted them as genuine 'fragments of
ancient Gaelic poetry', and some (like Boswell's friend Thomas
Sheridan) came to look upon them as 'the standard of feeling, . . . a
thermometer by which they could judge of the warmth of every-
body's heart'.[1] Dr. Johnson, it is true, thought them an imposture,
and did not hesitate to say so. The dispute about their authenticity,
however, did not affect their vogue on the Continent; the Preface
to a new edition, 'carefully corrected, and greatly improved'
(London, 1773), refers with satisfaction to 'the eagerness with which
these Poems have been received abroad' as providing 'a recompence
for the coldness with which a few have affected to treat them at
home'. In the same year, Herder, resolutely stifling all doubts about
their origins, published his famous essay *Über Ossian und die Lieder
alter Völker.* In 1774 the sensational success of Goethe's *Werther*
added further fuel to the flames: as the thought of suicide takes
possession of the hero's tortured mind, he finds in *Ossian* the kind of
reading that suits his mood of despair. Like other young men who
were infected, more or less temporarily, with Werther's *taedium
vitae,* Schiller too had revelled in the brooding melancholy of Ossian
at an early age. Evidence of his familiarity with the poems first
appears in January 1779, when, at the age of nineteen, he was called
upon to deliver a formal oration in the presence of Duke Karl
Eugen of Suabia, the founder and patron of the Military Academy
where he was being educated. The subject of his speech was
Virtue; the occasion the birthday of the Duke's mistress. In this
address, which culminates in an encomium on the Duke, he draws
upon the first Book of *Temora* for an example of noble-minded
modesty: 'The light of heaven was in the bosom of Cathmor. . . .
But Cathmor dwelt in the wood, to shun the voice of praise!'

Schiller's correspondence shows that his interest in the Ossianic
poems was no mere passing craze. In his circle of acquaintance,

[1] Boswell's *London Journal,* February 8, 1763.

Ossian was evidently a name to conjure with. Two of his friends, F. von Hoven and J. W. Petersen, published translations of *Ossian*, and it has been plausibly suggested that Schiller's own poem *Hektors Abschied* owes something to Hoven's rendering of *Carric-Thura*.[1] Ossianic allusions came readily to Schiller's mind: commenting on Hoven's shortcomings as a correspondent, he remarks, in a letter to Petersen (July 1, 1784): 'Hovens Stimme ist verhallet in Selma"— an echo from *The Songs of Selma*. Later on, in the days of his court-ship, he was delighted to discover that his future wife, Charlotte von Lengefeld, was a devotee of Ossian. 'I am glad to see that you are remaining faithful to this fine poet', he writes in a letter of January 3, 1789. On another occasion (March 26, 1789), he speaks of the bard's gift of infusing his own feelings into nature, and adds, with special reference to *Dar-Thula*: 'I am happy to revive through you the memory of one of the most delightful moments of my youth.' Charlotte had translated the *Death of Cuthullin* and some other pieces; it goes without saying that Schiller, reading these translations with a lover's eye, proved a benevolent critic. Nor did his renewed interest in *Ossian* fail to leave its traces on his own poetic work: he makes a point of explaining to his friend G. Körner that a passage in *Die Künstler*—one of his major reflective poems, written at that time—is based on a simile borrowed from *Ossian* (March 30, 1789).

One of Schiller's most fruitful (and most controversial) contribu-tions to modern criticism is contained in his essay *Über naive und sentimentalische Dichtung* (1795–96), where he characterizes what we should now call 'romantic' literature. Once again he invokes the shade of Ossian, and again we see how formative an experience his early enthusiasm for the Ossianic poems had been. He holds them up as a model of elegiac poetry; he speaks admiringly of their power and their idealizing tendency, as exemplified, for instance, in 'that excellent poem, *Carthon*'. Describing Goethe's *Werther* as a 'romantic' subject treated by a 'naïve' author, he says:

It is interesting to observe with what happy instinctive skill everything that fosters the romantic character is blended in *Werther*: ecstatic and unhappy love, a feeling for nature, religious emotions, the spirit of philosophical contemplation, and finally—so as not to leave out anything—the gloomy, formless, melancholy Ossianic world.

More than thirty years later, Goethe said to Eckermann, with

[1] Cf. L. M. Price, *English-German Literary Influences* (Berkeley, 1919), p. 262. (I have not been able to consult the article by W. Fielitz which Price quotes.)

explicit reference to Schiller's essay: 'The notion of classical and romantic poetry, which is now spreading all over the world and causing so much controversy and division, originated with myself and Schiller' (March 21, 1830). Remembering that his contact with 'the formless, melancholy Ossianic world' was one of the earliest of those adventures among books which helped to evolve the idea of romantic literature in Schiller's mind, we can gauge the importance of the Ossianic influence—even if Goethe's remark be taken with the appropriate pinch of salt.

In the same essay Schiller refers briefly to another Scottish poet who was widely read and much esteemed in Germany: James Thomson. Schiller first read him in 1789, when a friend, Ludwig Schubart, sent him his new translation of *The Seasons*. (The poem had been translated before, in 1745, by B. H. Brockes.) He was favourably impressed, but in *Über naive und sentimentalische Dichtung* he has nothing original to say on the matter; he merely likens Thomson to Ewald von Kleist, as a poet who excels in evoking moods suggested by rural scenes, but who is weak when he attempts to portray human beings and their actions.

While Schiller was writing *Don Carlos*—a long and complex play, slow to take shape—he gradually acquired a fairly extensive knowledge of the reigns of Philip II of Spain and of his father, Charles V. These historical studies, first undertaken as a means to an end, finally became an end in themselves. 'My affection for history grows daily. . . . I wish I had studied nothing but history for ten years running', he confesses in a letter to Körner (April 15, 1786); and presently his background studies for *Don Carlos* produced an offshoot in the shape of his *History of the Revolt of the Netherlands* (1788). Though he found this essay in history a far less exacting task than his play had been, it was more favourably received by the public. Wieland, still one of the most influential critics of the day, encouraged him in the belief that the writing of history was his true vocation. When, through Goethe's good offices, Schiller was offered a professorship of history in the University of Jena, he accepted (although the post was far from being a lucrative one), and for some time the study, the teaching, and the writing of history became his main professional occupations.

As one reads Schiller's correspondence, one cannot resist the impression that Scottish influence had something to do with this new departure. Among contemporary works on the period of

Spanish history that was engrossing Schiller's attention, the contributions of Scottish historians took pride of place. There was the *History of Charles V* (1769, translated into German in 1770–71) by the celebrated Dr. William Robertson; and there was the *History of Philip II* by Robert Watson, Professor of Philosophy and Rhetoric in the University of St. Andrews, and later Principal of the United Colleges of St. Salvator and St. Leonard's in that University. Both figure in Schiller's letters. At a time when he was still struggling with the 'chaotic mass' of *Don Carlos*, he tells his friend F. Huber (October 5, 1785): 'I am deep in Watson just now, and important changes are in store for my Philip and Alva.' It has been suggested, by the editor of Schiller's historical writings in one of the standard editions of his works, that it was Watson's book which prompted Schiller to embark upon his own *History of the Revolt of the Netherlands*.[1] If that is so, the Scottish Professor may be said to have exercised a decisive influence at a critical moment in Schiller's life, for it was his *History of the Revolt of the Netherlands* that furnished him with the requisite credentials for his appointment to a Chair of History. We know, at any rate, that in Schiller's eyes the prestige of an historian like William Robertson was a strong argument in favour of history as a career. In a letter to Körner, who wanted his friend to concentrate his energies on his work as a poet and dramatist, and feared that he might be side-tracked by the pursuit of history, he writes (January 7, 1788): 'While people admire a great poet, they venerate a man like Robertson—and if that same Robertson had written in a poetic spirit, people would venerate as well as admire him.' (Coming across a remark like this, a 'scientific' historian of the present day would probably raise a mocking eyebrow; but his amusement, understandable as it may be from his point of view, would not be shared in all quarters of his own profession, or by all modern philosophers of history. G. M. Trevelyan, for instance, has given it as his opinion that 'the motive of history is at bottom poetic', and R. G. Collingwood has expressed similar views.[2]) 'Who can assert', Schiller continues, 'that I may not be able to do that some day . . .?' In turning historian, Schiller was emulating Robertson, and hoping to surpass him.

Robertson's name first occurs in Schiller's correspondence in December 1782, in a list of books which Schiller wished to borrow

---

[1] Richard Fester, in the 'Säkular-Ausgabe' of Schiller's works, vol. 14, p. 421.

[2] G. M. Trevelyan, *History and the Reader* (London, 1945), p. 18; R. G. Collingwood, *The Idea of History* (Oxford, 1946), p. 245.

from the library at Meiningen; one of the titles he requested was Robertson's *History of Scotland.* (It is interesting to note that in a list consisting of twenty items, no fewer than six are works by Scottish authors. Scottish philosophy is represented by Home's *Elements of Criticism*, by Adam Smith's *Theory of Moral Sentiments*, and by the essays on *Genius* and *Taste* by Alexander Gerard, Professor of Moral Philosophy at Aberdeen; Scottish historiography by Robertson and Hume.) Schiller must have read the *History of Scotland* to some purpose, for about three months later the idea of a play on the subject of Mary Queen of Scots crops up in several letters. The project was shelved, but remained unforgotten. Five years later (March 1788), when he was immersed in his historical studies, he sent a copy of Robertson's book to Charlotte von Lengefeld, with the injunction: 'Let your heart be touched by the suffering of the poor Queen.' Another dozen years elapsed before Schiller the playwright returned to the story of 'the poor Queen'; but return to it he did, and his tragedy *Maria Stuart* (1801) remains one of the best, and one of the best loved, of his later plays.

Like the Scottish historians, the 'Scottish School' of philosophy had its adherents in Germany. Its European reputation created a demand for translations; Francis Hutcheson's *Inquiry into the Original of our Ideas of Beauty and Virtue* (translated by Goethe's friend J. H. Merck—'Mephistopheles Merck', as Goethe used to call him), Thomas Reid's *Inquiry into the Human Mind on the Principles of Common Sense*, Adam Ferguson's *Institutes of Moral Philosophy*, Henry Home's *Elements of Criticism* were all available in German. Many German students of philosophy sat at the feet of teachers who had been profoundly influenced by these Scottish thinkers. Schiller's teacher Jakob Friedrich Abel is an example. Abel was an eclectic; the elements of the system which he expounded to his students were derived from sources which included the Scottish School; and it was mainly through his teaching that the views of the School—and more particularly those of Adam Ferguson—came to affect Schiller. This influence can be seen in the speech on *Virtue considered in its consequences* which has been mentioned before. When Schiller speaks of an 'eternal law' which establishes a correlation between individual happiness and the perfection of society, and which therefore causes men to take pleasure in whatever contributes to social progress and the common good, he is echoing certain pronouncements on the 'Laws of the Will' in which Ferguson asserts that man's desire for excellence 'is an ultimate fact in the nature of man, and not to be explained by anything that is previously or better known', and that 'men naturally desire the welfare of their fellow-creatures'.[1] When, in the same speech, Schiller extols universal love as the bond that unites all men and sustains their spiritual life, a ruling principle in the realm of the spirit, like the law of gravitation in the physical world (we recognize one of the sources of the famous *Ode to Joy*), he is again re-stating, in much more rhetorical language, what Ferguson had propounded: that 'the greatest good competent to man's nature, is the love of mankind', and 'that there is no happiness of the part consistent with what is hurtful to the whole'.[2]

The same views are advanced in the extant fragment of Schiller's unsuccessful first thesis, *Philosophy of Physiology*. Taking it for granted that this world, planned by a divine intelligence, must be the best of possible worlds, he asserts that to survey the purposes of divine providence is supreme bliss. The 'contemporary sage' whom he quotes in support is none other than Ferguson, who holds that 'the affection of a mind enlightened to conceive what is the object and what the efficacy of God's providence, is, of all others, most pleasant, and approaches most to an entire exemption from pain'.[3]

These reassuring glimpses of a pre-established harmony between enlightened self-interest and the public weal, of a life irradiated by general altruism, with common sense and good taste as man's safe guides in his progress towards the twin ideals of moral and aesthetic excellence, bring to mind Shaftesbury's 'virtuoso-science' and his concept of 'moral grace'. The Scottish philosophers, and more especially Hutcheson and Ferguson, provided a channel through which Shaftesbury's ideas reached Germany, where they found congenial and enthusiastic interpreters such as Wieland and Herder, and where Shaftesbury's name continued to be held in high esteem long after it had suffered an almost total eclipse at home. Inasmuch as Schiller absorbed elements of Shaftesbury's thought through the teaching of Ferguson, his early contact with the Scottish School must be regarded as a major factor in his development; for certain features of Shaftesbury's doctrine—his belief in a close connection between man's aesthetic sensibility and his moral disposition, the importance which he attaches to aesthetic experience, and his

---

[1] *Institutes of Moral Philosophy* (Edinburgh, 1769), pt. ii, ch. ii, pp. 95 and 91.
[2] Ibid., pt. iv, ch. v, pp. 171–72.
[3] *Institutes of Moral Philosophy* (Edinburgh, 1769), pt. iv, ch. iii, p. 154.

conviction that the harmonious development of the individual will benefit the community—became and remained fundamental in Schiller's own thought, although at a later stage Shaftesbury's somewhat facile optimism seemed to him to stand in need of qualification.

That qualification he derived from Kant, who was the other main influence in Schiller's development as a thinker. Kant had stressed the uniqueness of moral experience, and had formulated his concept of the categorical imperative of duty with what seemed to Schiller unnecessary rigour. With Shaftesbury, Schiller insists—against Kant's rigorism—that a good man will often do his duty, not slavishly, under the lash of harsh compulsion, but freely, cheerfully, and without any inward struggle, because it seems the natural and the most satisfying thing to do. On the other hand, he is well aware that there are occasions, all too common in human experience, when the performance of one's duty necessarily entails sacrifice and suffering. If at such times a man chooses to obey the 'categorical imperative', he must try to do with dignity what he can no longer do easily and gracefully. Schiller formulated these ideas in an essay which is one of the best examples of his philosophical prose, and which by its very title—*Über Anmut und Würde* (*On Grace and Dignity*)—proclaims his position between Shaftesbury and Kant. In developing the implications of the title, linking Shaftesbury's 'virtuoso-science' with Kant's ethic, Schiller gives fresh meaning and precision to well-known and well-worn terms. Henry Home, for instance, suggests the antithesis of dignity and grace in his *Elements of Criticism*, but he does not work it out very clearly. Schiller was familiar with Home's book—he possessed a copy of his own—and he must have regarded it as a work of some value, for he urged his friend Körner to produce a new translation of it (May 25, 1792). In *Über Anmut und Würde* he twice mentions it in footnotes, and although both notes express disagreement, they show, at any rate, that the book was in Schiller's mind at the time, and that he was disposed to take it more seriously than did Dr. Johnson, whom Boswell reports as remarking (at their very first meeting): 'Sir, this book is a pretty essay, and deserves to be held in some estimation, though much of it is chimerical.'[1]

An inventory of Schiller's debt to Scottish writers reflects, on the one hand, the range of Schiller's mind and the variety of his

---

[1] The same comment, worded more trenchantly ('though it is chimerical'), is reported in Boswell's *London Journal*, May 16, 1763.

interests; and, on the other, the vigour and diversity of Scottish literary culture in Schiller's day. It will be noticed that two major figures of his own generation do not come into the picture. It is doubtful whether Schiller would have been able to appreciate Burns, had he known about him; he certainly could not have savoured the rich characteristic bouquet of his language. As for Scott, one may conjecture that Schiller would have liked him very much; but Scott appeared on the scene just too late to engage his attention. Even so, a survey such as this suggests that the sum-total of Scottish influence on Schiller was greater, and of greater moment, than is commonly realized.

III

TIME IN *WALLENSTEIN* AND *MACBETH*

WALLENSTEIN and *Macbeth* have several salient features in common. Both plays tell a story of 'vaulting ambition, which o'erleaps itself'. The heroes of both dramas commit crimes in order to gain the power they crave; but they do so reluctantly, shrinking from the means while desiring the end: they are both men who 'would not play false, and yet would wrongly win'. Both are urged on, at a critical moment, by strong-willed women whose singleness of purpose prevails over all misgivings and scruples. In both tragedies the champions of the traditional order close their ranks against the usurper, and finally lay him low. Even the 'supernatural soliciting' of the witches, their prediction of royal hope which Macbeth construes as an incitement to murder, may be said to have a parallel in the favourable conjunction of the planets which Wallenstein interprets as a call to action.

References to *Macbeth* in some of Schiller's earliest writings[1] show how strongly the play had appealed to his youthful mind. His response deepened as the years went by. In his correspondence *Macbeth* is mentioned more often than any other work of Shakespeare's. When the plan of *Wallenstein* was taking shape in his mind, he explicitly invoked the example of *Macbeth* to justify the projected design of his own play.[2] When *Wallenstein* was finished, the fascination of Shakespeare's tragedy remained, prompting him, in the early months of the year 1800, to write his adaptation of *Macbeth* for the Weimar theatre. There can be no doubt that the two works were closely linked in Schiller's mind. No commentary on his adaptation of *Macbeth* would be complete without extensive reference to *Wallenstein*, and no editor of *Wallenstein* could fail to mention *Macbeth*. Yet, even though the parallel between the two plays belongs to the stock-in-trade of dramatic criticism, the subject is by no means exhausted. It may be worth-while to seek a fresh approach to it by asking how time enters into the experience— conscious as well as subconscious—of the protagonists. With what sense of time are Wallenstein and Macbeth endowed by their

---

[1] Cf. his thesis *Über den Zusammenhang der tierischen Natur des Menschen mit seiner geistigen*, Section 26; *Über das gegenwärtige teutsche Theater*; and the original Preface to *Die Räuber*.
[2] Letter to Goethe, November 28, 1796.

creators?[1] In what follows, three aspects of that question will be considered: (1) time and eternity; (2) time as an element in the order of nature and society; and (3) time as a condition of human action.

The familiar contrast between time and eternity, with all its religious associations, must inevitably loom large in plays dealing with guilt and retribution. We think of eternity (in so far as we can think of it at all) not as a mere extension of time, but as a different mode or dimension of existence. We say that God has His being in eternity, outside time and beyond it; and such intimations of immortality as may be granted to some men suggest that the life of the human soul is not wholly governed by time either: they 'have power to make our noisy years seem moments in the being of the eternal Silence'. The belief in the immortality of the soul has obvious eschatological implications: it entails the question of the soul's fate in the hereafter.

Both Wallenstein and Macbeth revolve these matters in their minds. In order to gain their ends, both men have to break a sacred trust, and both realize the enormity of the crime they are contemplating. They know that in order to attain the power they covet, they must come to terms with the forces of evil. Macbeth, thinking of Duncan, speaks of 'the deep damnation of his taking-off'; soon after the murder he laments the loss of his 'eternal jewel' which he has 'given to the common Enemy of man'. Wallenstein expresses similar thoughts:

> Den Edelstein, das allgeschätzte Gold
> Muß man den falschen Mächten abgewinnen,
> Die unterm Tage schlimmgeartet hausen.
> Nicht ohne Opfer macht man sie geneigt,
> Und keiner lebt, der aus ihrem Dienst
> Die Seele hätte rein zurückgezogen.[2]

Both men are warned against those devilish powers—Wallenstein by Max Piccolomini, Macbeth by Banquo, who reminds him that the instruments of Darkness may 'win us with honest trifles, to betray's in deepest consequence'. They both assert, however, that if only they could be sure of success in this world, the world of time,

---

[1] This kind of inquiry differs in emphasis, as it does in scope, from those carried out in such works as Emil Staiger's *Die Zeit als Einbildungskraft des Dichters* (Zurich, 1939) or G. Poulet's *Études sur le temps humain* (Edinburgh, 1949).

[2] The jewel, the all-valued gold we win
From the deceiving Powers, depraved in nature,
That dwell beneath the day and blessed sun-light.
Not without sacrifices are they rendered
Propitious, and there lives no soul on earth
That e'er retired unsullied from their service.

(Coleridge's translation)

they would accept the risk of damnation in the world to come. Wallenstein, likening himself to Caesar crossing the Rubicon, dismisses his young friend's entreaties with the words

> Gib mir sein Glück, das andre will ich tragen.[1]

Macbeth puts it even more plainly, in a famous passage:

> . . . if th'assassination
> Could trammel up the consequence, and catch
> With his surcease success; that but this blow
> Might be the be-all and the end-all—here,
> But here, upon this bank and shoal of time,
> We'd jump the life to come.

It might appear, then, as if the two heroes' thoughts and feelings about time and eternity were essentially the same. But that is not so: the analogies which have been noted cloak a vital difference. When Wallenstein declares that he is not disposed to worry about the danger threatening his soul in the hereafter, that assertion expresses his real state of mind and is borne out by his subsequent behaviour. It is true that his mind is troubled before and at the moment of crisis (though even then he is not thinking in absolute terms of right and wrong, good and evil: his qualms of conscience blend with considerations of expediency). But once he is committed to his act of treason, all these compunctions leave him; while some members of his *entourage* are visited by sinister forebodings, Wallenstein himself remains confident and strangely serene. What a contrast—Wallenstein who, in his final scene, looks forward to a long night's rest after the strain of the last few days; and the Thane of Glamis who has murdered sleep, whose mind is full of scorpions, and who, soon after his deed, has come to envy his victim:

> Better be with the dead,
> Whom we, to gain our peace, have sent to peace,
> Than on the torture of the mind to lie
> In restless ecstasy.

Macbeth tries to do what Wallenstein succeeds in doing—to concentrate upon questions of immediate policy and to dismiss all thoughts of eternity; but he fails. The voice of his conscience is not to be silenced. It has been argued that by killing Duncan, Macbeth murders not sleep only but time as well; that for him time loses its meaning, ceases to function,[2] and that he enters into the kind of time-

---

[1] Give me his luck, that other thing I'll bear.

[2] Cf. J. Middleton Murry, *Shakespeare*, London, 1936, pp. 331 ff.; Mark van Doren, *Shakespeare*, London, 1941, pp. 261 ff.; G. Wilson Knight, *The Imperial Theme*, 3rd ed., London, 1951, p. 150; Edith Sitwell, *A Notebook on William Shakespeare*, London, 1948, pp. 25 f.; Roy Walker, *The Time is Free*, London, 1949, pp. ix, 76, 190.

less torment which Marlowe's Mephistophilis describes to Faustus:

> Hell hath no limits, nor is circumscrib'd
> In one self place; for where we are is hell,
> And where hell is, there must we ever be . . .

Judgment has come: 'And the angel . . . sware by him that liveth
for ever and ever . . . that there should be time no longer.'[1] Before
his crime, Macbeth hopes that the horror of it will pass:

> Come what come may,
> Time and the hour runs through the roughest day.

But once the deed is done, he finds that he cannot put it behind
him, as he had hoped to do, but that he must live with it always.
When the murder has been discovered, and Macbeth, feigning
grief, exclaims

> Had I but died an hour before this chance,
> I had liv'd a blessed time . . .

we know that with terrible irony Shakespeare makes him state the
truth in the very act of dissembling. And the same is true of the
murder of Banquo: again Macbeth's crime, in the shape of Banquo's
ghost, insists on staying with him; half beside himself with terror,
he realizes how time has ceased to operate, how the past refuses to
remain past:

> . . . the time has been,
> That, when the brains were out, the man would die,
> And there an end; but now, they rise again . . .

The play, as a recent editor remarks, 'is about damnation';[2] the
action and the hero are seen *sub specie aeternitatis*, transcending time.
Wallenstein, on the other hand, for all his imposing stature, remains
a creature of time whose hopes and fears are centred in this world.

The passage of time is felt to be of the essence of all human
experience; indeed, the ordinary man cannot conceive of existence
outside time, although glimpses of such a mode of being may now
and then be vouchsafed to the mystic.[3] Time enters into the most
intimate data of our individual consciousness—our heart-beat,
the rhythm of our breathing—and we cannot describe the course or
the setting of our lives without using words that imply the notion
of time: birth, growth, decay, day and night, the seasons of the year,

---

[1] Revelation x. 5–6.

[2] Kenneth Muir in the Introduction to his edition of *Macbeth*, London, 1951, p. li.

[3] 'Die Seele berührt mit ihren höchsten Kräften die Ewigkeit, das ist Gott, und mit den
niedersten Kräften die Zeit. · · Selig und am seligsten sind die, die da über Zeit und Raum
und Form und Materie in das ewige Jetzt sich gestellt haben . . . (Eckhart; modernized version by A. Bernt).

seed and harvest. 'To every thing there is a season, and a time to every purpose under the heaven: A time to be born, and a time to die; a time to plant, and a time to pluck up that which is planted.' Time thus comes to be regarded as part of the order of nature, and, by extension, of human society, since it is essential to the conception of any social or political order. Language shows how deeply these ideas are embedded in our habits of thought: we speak of 'the test of time', of 'venerable old age', of 'time-honoured' customs and institutions, and the lawyer is familiar with the notion of 'use and wont' establishing legal rights.

In pursuing their ambition, Wallenstein and Macbeth both violate a moral and political order sanctified by time. Wallenstein, more reflective (though less imaginative) than Macbeth, analyses the nature of his undertaking.

> Und was ist dein Beginnen? Hast du dirs
> Auch redlich selbst bekannt?

he asks himself, and proceeds to give the answer:

> Du willst die Macht,
> Die ruhig, sicher thronende erschüttern,
> Die in verjährt geheiligtem Besitz,
> In der Gewohnheit festgegründet ruht . . .[1]

Here lies the real danger; what is old is felt to be sacred—

> Das *Jahr* übt eine heiligende Kraft;
> Was grau für Alter ist, das ist ihm göttlich.
> Sei im Besitze, und du wohnst im Recht,
> Und heilig wirds die Menge dir bewahren.[2]

In *Macbeth* this idea is conveyed less explicitly, but no less clearly. Duncan, the embodiment of the order which Macbeth seeks to destroy, the king to whom he owes allegiance, the kinsman to whom he is bound by ties of blood, the guest for whose safety he is responsible, is an old man; an old man, moreover, who traces his descent back in time through a line of legitimate rulers. His body is

> Carried to Colme-kill,[3]
> The sacred storehouse of his predecessors,
> And guardian of their bones.

---

[1] What is thy enterprise? thy aim? thy object?
Power seated on a quiet throne thou'dst shake,
Power on an ancient consecrated throne,
Strong in possession, founded in old custom.

[2]   For time consecrates;
And what is grey with age becomes religion.
Be in possession, and thou hast the right,
And sacred will the many guard it for thee!

[3] I.e. Iona.

The nation's wholesome days under Duncan are contrasted with the usurper's reign, when the frame of things is disjointed, and all that happens is unnatural 'even like the deed that's done'. It is not until that unnatural reign ends with the tyrant's death that a saner order of government and society can be restored, and Macduff can announce that 'the time is free'.

It has often been observed that *Macbeth*, the shortest of the great tragedies, is the one that moves fastest. This sense of speed is felt from the start; in a letter to Goethe (April 25, 1797), Schiller specially notes that the exposition in *Macbeth*, while acquainting us with the antecedents of the plot, advances the action at the same time. There is no pause in the feverish rush of events until we come to the concluding scene of Act IV. In all these respects *Wallenstein* is the exact opposite of *Macbeth*. It is the longest of Schiller's dramatic works (nearly four times as long as *Macbeth*), and it contains a large amount of retarding expository matter. It moves slowly at first, and does not gather speed until it has run more than half its long course.

And yet, in spite of these differences in length, in pace, and in the variations of pace, the two plays show a marked resemblance at the moment of climax, which is reached when the hero makes his decision. In both cases, the greatest possible stress is laid upon the significance of that moment. Both heroes feel it to be crucial. Wallenstein speaks of 'the parting of the ways'; looking at the threshold which will presently be crossed by the Swedish envoy, he remarks:

> Noch ist sie rein — noch! Das Verbrechen kam
> Nicht über diese Schwelle noch — So schmal ist
> Die Grenze, die zwei Lebenspfade scheidet![1]

Both men falter, and would for a moment like to draw back.

> Hört! Noch ist nichts geschehn, und — wohl erwogen,
> Ich will es lieber doch nicht tun[2]

says Wallenstein after the Swede has left. Macbeth's reflections lead to the same conclusion:

> We will proceed no further in this business.

In both cases, this impulse passes. Wallenstein sends for the Swedish

[1] Yet is it pure—as yet!—the crime has come
   Not o'er this threshold yet—so slender is
   The boundary that divideth life's two paths.
[2] As yet is nothing settled: and (well weighed)
   I feel myself inclined to leave it so

plenipotentiary in order to ratify his treasonable pact with the enemy, and Macbeth resolves upon murder with the words

> I am settled, and bend up
> Each corporal agent to this terrible feat.

Once again, however, these outward similarities veil an underlying difference. Without doubt Macbeth is impelled to his deed by potent influences. There is his own ambitious nature; there is the witches' prophecy;[1] there is, above all, his wife's inflexible determination. But great as the psychological pressure may be, there is nothing in the external, material circumstances that can be said to make the decision inevitable. No one knows anything about his murderous thoughts except his wife; and although Lady Macbeth might despise him if he flinched from his purpose, she would never give him away. Their dreams of royal power have not yet issued in any action that commits them. 'Art thou afeard' (Lady Macbeth asks)

> To be the same in thine own act and valour
> As thou art in desire?

She may say to her husband

> Thy letters have transported me beyond
> This ignorant present, and I feel now
> The future in the instant;

but for all that, the future is in the balance, and depends on Macbeth's decision. Time, then, is here conceived as a (discontinuous) succession of instants each one of which may be considered separately, each one of which may bring a decision, and each one of which might therefore mark a new beginning.

In his Notes on *Macbeth*, Coleridge inserts a reference to that central scene in *Wallenstein* which Goethe called the 'axis of the play'—the long soliloquy in which the hero meditates upon his situation while awaiting the Swedish emissary.[2] Coleridge observes that Macbeth's mind has been 'rendered *temptable* by previous dalliance of the fancy with ambitious thoughts', and this comment echoes several passages from Wallenstein's great monologue:

> Wärs möglich? Könnt ich nicht mehr, wie ich wollte?
> Nicht mehr zurück, wie mirs beliebt? Ich müßte
> Die Tat *vollbringen*, weil ich sie *gedacht*,
> Nicht die Versuchung von mir wies — das Herz

---

[1] It must be remembered, however, that 'the murder is not preordained, though Macbeth's rule as king may be'. (Peter Alexander, *Shakespeare's Life and Art*, London, 1939, p. 172.)

[2] *Coleridge's Shakespearean Criticism*, ed. by T. M. Raysor, vol. I, London, 1930, p. 68.

Genährt mit diesem Traum, auf ungewisse
Erfüllung hin die Mittel mir gespart,
Die Wege bloß mir offen hab gehalten? —
....
Wars unrecht, an dem Gaukelbilde mich
Der königlichen Hoffnung zu ergötzen?[1]

Coleridge, it would appear, considered that what he was saying about Macbeth applied to Wallenstein too. But does it? Surely Wallenstein's speech, taken in its dramatic context, conveys something more, and something rather different. It is not simply a question of Wallenstein's mind having become 'temptable' by his indulgence in secret dreams of power. The point is, rather, that the 'previous dalliance of the fancy with ambitious thoughts' has, through its influence on his personality and his conduct, affected the external situation in which he now finds himself.

Blieb in der Brust mir nicht der Wille frei,
Und sah ich nicht den guten Weg zur Seite,
Der mir die Rückkehr offen stets bewahrte?
Wohin denn seh ich plötzlich mich geführt?
Bahnlos liegts hinter mir, und eine Mauer
Aus meinen eignen Werken baut sich auf,
Die mir die Rückkehr türmend hemmt!
Strafbar erschein ich, und ich kann die Schuld,
Wie ichs versuchen mag! nicht von mir wälzen;
Denn mich verklagt der Doppelsinn des Lebens . . .[2]

Wallenstein had thought that a man's secret hopes and wishes can somehow be kept apart from what we call 'the outside world'. He now recognizes that this was a mistake—that the so-called

[1]   Is it possible?
Is't so? I can no longer what I would?
No longer draw back at my liking? I
Must do the deed, because I thought of it,
And fed this heart here with a dream? Because
I did not scowl temptation from my presence,
Dallied with thoughts of possible fulfilment . . .?
        . . . Was it criminal
To make the fancy minister to hope . . .
And clutch fantastic sceptres moving t'ward me?
[2] Was not the will kept free? Beheld I not
The road of duty close beside me—but
One little step, and once more I was in it!
Where am I? Whither have I been transported?
No road, no track behind me, but a wall,
Impenetrable, insurmountable,
Rises obedient to the spells I muttered
And meant not—my own doings tower behind me.
A punishable man I seem, the guilt,
Try what I will, I cannot roll off from me;
The equivocal demeanour of my life
Bears witness on my prosecutor's party . . .

'outside world' and our inner world of thoughts and feelings constantly interact, and that what happens in one affects and conditions the other.

> In meiner Brust war meine Tat noch mein[1]

he says—and the past tense is significant: he knows that he is no longer free to choose. When, earlier on in the play, his henchmen press for a decision, Wallenstein puts them off with the words

> Die Zeit ist noch nicht da.[2]

Terzky replies impatiently

> So sagst du immer.
> Wann aber wird es Zeit sein?[3]

And Wallenstein rejoins:

> Wenn ichs sage.[4]

He believes, at that stage, that he can as it were intersect the flow of time, marking out one particular moment, which shall be the moment of decision. Yet throughout the play we are made to realize that Wallenstein's notion of time and human action is false, that time is indivisible, and that the decision which he projected into the future belongs to the past: 'that which is to be hath already been'. The ambiguity of his former conduct, his tentative preparations, are now seen to have been decisive: past events acquire their context and their significance in the light of subsequent developments. Wallenstein wanted to leave his intentions fluid, but he finds that such a state of indeterminacy, of non-commitment, cannot be prolonged, and that it may end at a time and under circumstances which are not of one's own choosing.

Psychologically and philosophically,[5] this is an interesting and subtle conception, and Schiller develops it with great skill. Dramatically, on the other hand, it is less telling than the more clear-cut choice that confronts Macbeth.[6]

While he is under the delusion that events will wait his leisure, Wallenstein, speaking of the conditions of human action in time,

---

[1] My deed was mine, remaining in my bosom   [2] The time is not yet come.
[3]   So you say always.   [4] When I shall say it.
     But when will it be time?
[5] Cf. Bergson's celebrated distinction between the factitious, spatialized time of the clock and the creative unfolding which he calls '*durée réelle*'.
[6] Coleridge felt this. In a manuscript note on *Wallenstein*, he remarks that 'Wallenstein is a finer psychological than dramatic, and a more dramatic than a tragic character' (*The Poetical Works of S. T. Coleridge*, ed. by E. H. C., London, 1912, p. 599). But the reasoning with which he supports that view is not in his happiest vein.

uses the metaphor of seed-time and harvest:[1] to achieve the desired result, one must sow at the right moment. As the play moves towards its close, the deceptiveness of that analogy is brought home to him. What he learns to his cost—that men are always sowing the seeds of the future, that growth is continuous, and the season of fruition unpredictable—was summed up by Schiller in a later play:[2]

> *Aber nichts ist verloren und verschwunden,*
> *Was die geheimnisvoll waltenden Stunden*
> *In den dunkel schaffenden Schoß aufnahmen—*
> *Die Zeit ist eine blühende Flur,*
> *Ein großes Lebendiges ist die Natur,*
> *Und alles ist Frucht, und alles ist Samen.*

There is a striking passage in the fourth chapter of the Gospel according to St. John in which the same kind of imagery is used in regard to time. In the context of a more sublime drama, it serves to correct a misconception not unlike that which Wallenstein has to unlearn:

'Say not ye, There are yet four months, and then cometh harvest? behold, I say unto you, Lift up your eyes, and look on the fields; for they are white already to harvest.'

---

[1] *Die Piccolomini*, II, vi, 986 ff.   [2] *Die Braut von Messina*, III, v. 1998 ff.

IV

WARBECK AND *DEMETRIUS*

AMONG the dramatic fragments and sketches which Schiller left behind, two—*Perkin Warbeck* and *Demetrius*—stand out from the rest. These two projects, which had engaged Schiller's attention during the last years of his life, and which had progressed further than any of the others, are closely linked by similarity of theme. In both dramas the central figure is a pretender to a royal title; both depict the hero's attempt to assert his claim.

Perkin Warbeck comes first in chronological order. As early as 1799, when Schiller was writing *Maria Stuart* and when British history was therefore much in his mind, he told Goethe[1] that he had come across a subject for a new play—the story of the impostor who sought to dispute Henry VII's title to the crown of England, basing his claim on the allegation that he was Richard, Duke of York, the younger son of Edward IV, that he had escaped death when Tyrell came to murder the Princes in the Tower, and that he was thus the rightful heir to the throne. Schiller points out how a situation of this kind could be made the subject either of comedy or of tragedy. To achieve a comic effect the playwright would have to present the principal character as being ludicrously unfitted for the exalted position to which he aspires. In a tragedy, on the other hand, the protagonist would have to appear as a man cast by nature for the role which he wants to play, his spirit and royal bearing matching his pretensions. Schiller goes on to say that the catastrophe in such a play would arise from the hero's refusal to be a mere tool in the hands of his supporters. It would, in fact, be the tragedy of a man who comes to grief because, though born with all the attributes of a king, he was not born a king.

Schiller cannot have known that he had been forestalled by an English dramatist of the Caroline period. Had he read John Ford's *Perkin Warbeck* (printed in 1634), he could not have failed to notice the analogies, as well as the differences, between Ford's treatment of the subject and his own conception of it. Ford liberally endows his hero with princely qualities—qualities which win him, for a time, a powerful ally in the person of King James IV of Scotland.

[1] Letter of August 20, 1799.

On first acquaintance, King James cannot resist the appeal of Warbeck's personality:

> He must be more than subject who can utter
> The language of a king, and such is thine

he exclaims (II, 1); and again (II, 3)

> How like a king he looks! Lords, but observe
> The confidence of his aspect; dross cannot
> Cleave to so pure a metal—royal youth!
> Plantagenet undoubted!

All this is completely in line with Schiller's notion of the part; but cutting across these similarities there is a cardinal difference. In Ford's play, Warbeck from first to last proudly upholds the validity of his claim. True, the author has given him no soliloquies and no asides, and it may therefore be argued that we are not told what goes on in his secret mind; nor do we learn on what evidence his claim is based. But if the playwright had meant us to suspect double-dealing, to surmise premeditated fraud behind a façade of perfectly consistent public utterance, he would surely have given some indication of this intention somewhere; for instance in the scene (IV, 2) in which the hero appears in conversation with his secretary and confidential agent, Stephen Frion. Yet here, as elsewhere, Warbeck insists emphatically on the justice of his cause, which, he asserts, remains unaffected by the success of Henry's policy:

> Let his mines
> Shap'd in the bowels of the earth, blow up
> Works rais'd for my defence, yet can they never
> Toss into air the freedom of my birth,
> Or disavow my blood Plantagenet's:
> I am my father's son still.

And when his secretary uses a turn of phrase which might be construed as casting some doubt upon his royal birth, Warbeck flares up.

> You grow too wild in passion [remarks Frion]: if you will
> Appear a prince indeed, confine your will
> To moderation;

whereupon Warbeck retorts vehemently

> What a saucy rudeness
> Prompts this distrust! If? If I will appear!
> Appear a prince! death throttle such deceits
> Even in their birth of utterance! cursèd cozenage
> Of trust! Ye make me mad: 'twere best, it seems,
> That I should turn impostor to myself,
> Be mine own counterfeit, belie the truth
> Of my dear mother's womb. . . .

He remains completely consistent in this attitude, even when disaster overtakes him. When he is a prisoner in the stocks, when death is staring him in the face, he still contemptuously rejects the advice offered him by Lambert Simnel, his predecessor in misfortune, who had sued for mercy and had been granted a pardon and a modest place as a falconer in the king's service. In accents of complete conviction, Warbeck declares that for him such a course would be unthinkable:

> Bread and a slavish ease, with some assurance
> From the base beadle's whip, crown'd all thy hopes:
> But, sirrah, ran there in thy veins one drop
> Of such a royal blood as flows in mine,
> Thou wouldst not change condition, to be second
> In England's state, without the crown itself. (V, 3)

Schiller's scenario and notes suggest an entirely different portrayal. In them Warbeck's enterprise is based on a deliberate fraud, though the dénouement of the play was apparently intended to show the hero in a more favourable light at the end. Refusing, as usual, to let the facts of recorded history cramp the free play of his poetic imagination, Schiller intended to make Warbeck a natural son of Edward IV. Thus his hero turns out to be a son of York after all, albeit born on the wrong side of the blanket; the blood of his ancestors (as Schiller puts it in his notes) 'works in him, obscurely but powerfully, and leads to actions which seem to be inconsistent with his role' (i.e. the role of an impostor).

It is doubtful, however, whether this motif—the secret, irresistible promptings of the royal blood, which, unknown to himself, flows in the hero's veins—could ever have reconciled us to the calculated fraud which forms the basis of the action. Throughout the greater part of the play, Warbeck would still have appeared as a cheat; the mainspring of the action would have been a rather shabby trick, and the hero's character would have been stained with a taint of meanness which nothing could quite obliterate. This proved a fatal flaw. Although Schiller's practice as a playwright was rather more flexible than his theory would lead one to expect, in that his later tragedies do not always conform to the conception of the sublime which he had set forth in his essays, a certain dignity, a greatness of spirit, remains a constant factor in the heroes of his plays. Such dignity is incompatible with the meanness of Warbeck's intrigue. There is evidence to show that this was one of the main reasons why Schiller shelved the subject again and again. He turned to it after he had finished *Die Jungfrau von Orleans*; but (as he explained to Körner)[1] he found that it refused to take shape; 'it is difficult to treat', he remarks, 'because the hero of the play is an impostor'. A few months later we find him still wrestling with it; 'but', he tells Körner,[2] 'the more closely I look at this play, the more the difficulties multiply'. Towards the end of his life, when he had started work on *Demetrius*, he drew up a kind of balance sheet, setting out the advantages and disadvantages of that subject as compared with *Warbeck*; and the first entry on the debit side of *Warbeck* is 'Fraud as a basis is repugnant'.

As a tragic hero, the impostor just would not do. Recognizing this, and holding himself free to deviate even further from historical fact, Schiller, loth to relinquish the subject altogether, thought of giving up the idea of a tragedy and of casting the play in a different mould. In his balance sheet, the 'happy ending' of *Warbeck* is explicitly mentioned as an item on the credit side. On that assumption, however, it is hard to see how the play would have ended, or indeed what it would have been about. Schiller was well aware of this difficulty, and his last two entries in the debit column state it plainly: 'No proper conclusion: No proper action.'

No one can say which of his various projects Schiller would have carried out, had he been spared; but it is a safe guess that if he had lived to complete *Demetrius*, he would not have returned to *Warbeck*. *Demetrius* supersedes *Warbeck*: it is *Warbeck* raised to a higher plane, and without the flaws of the earlier plan. The hero of the later work acts in good faith, at least to begin with; and his destiny unfolds itself, as Warbeck's does not, in stirring and spectacular scenes, full of movement and action.

When he sets out from Poland to march on Moscow, Demetrius believes in the justice of his cause. He is convinced that he is in fact a prince of the imperial house of Russia who has long been believed dead: Dmitri, the younger son of the late Czar Ivan the Terrible. Acting in that conviction, he takes the field against the usurper Boris Godunov, overthrows him, and makes himself master of Russia. At this point, at the height of success, he learns that he is not the true-born czarevitch at all. In the words of the title of a play which Schiller may be presumed to have known, Demetrius is 'A King and no King': ruler in fact, but not by right.

In 1785—the year in which Schiller left Mannheim in order to join C. G. Körner and his circle at Leipzig—his new friend Ludwig

---

[1] Letter of May 13, 1801.   [2] October 5, 1801.

Ferdinand Huber published what has been described as 'a tolerably close German adaptation'[1] of Beaumont's and Fletcher's play *A King and No King*, under the title *Ethelwolf oder Der König Kein König* (the scene being transferred from Armenia and Iberia to England and Scotland in Saxon times). Schiller twice refers to it in his letters,[2] and in view of the close personal relations that existed between him and Huber at that time, it seems not unreasonable to assume that he had at least glanced over Huber's version. What Schiller's *Demetrius* has in common with Beaumont's and Fletcher's play is the central situation of a hero who discovers, when he learns the secret of his descent, that he has no right to the royal power which he wields. There, however, the similarity ends. (It might conceivably be pointed out that Arane, the Queen Mother in Beaumont's and Fletcher's play, seeks the life of the hero who, contrary to the general belief, is not of her blood, and that Marfa, the Queen Mother in *Demetrius*, causes the hero's death when she refuses to recognize him as her son; but the analogy is too slight to merit much attention.) The discovery of the hero's parentage produces entirely different effects in the two plays: what turns out to be the salvation of Arbaces proves the ruin of Demetrius. Arbaces is overjoyed when he learns, at the end of the play, that he is not descended from the royal line, that the Princess Panthea, with whom he is passionately in love, is not his sister, and that his passion is therefore not an incestuous one. To be proved no king is, for him, 'the happiest news That e'er was heard', and he invites all and sundry to be partakers of his joy:

> Come, every one
> That takes delight in goodness, help to sing
> Loud thanks for me, that I am proved no King!

For Arbaces this revelation is the gateway to happiness; for Demetrius it is the beginning of the end. It robs him at one blow of his happy confidence in himself and in his cause, and it immediately leads to an act of criminal violence: mad with grief and rage, he kills the man who faked the evidence in support of his claim and who comes to demand his reward.

The episode of the *fabricator doli*, whose machinations launch Demetrius on his career, caused Schiller much searching of heart. The motivation—a deep-laid scheme of revenge—is rather far-fetched: the murderer of the true Demetrius raises up a false one

---

[1] R. Warwick Bond; Variorum edition of Beaumont's and Fletcher's works, vol. I, London, 1904, p. 247.

[2] To Körner, July 3, 1785, and to G. Göschen, April 7, 1786.

in order to get even with his double-crossing employer and accom-
plice. One cannot but agree with Kettner who remarks:[1] 'It is
ingeniously devised, certainly—only too ingeniously!' But if the
crisis of the play is engineered by somewhat artificial means, it
must on the other hand be granted that it creates a remarkably
pregnant situation. Up to this point Demetrius has been acting in
good faith. Now, when the great prize is within his grasp, he has
to decide, suddenly, without being given time for reflection,
whether he is to renounce his pretensions and fade into obscurity,
or whether he is to go on with his undertaking, in the knowledge
that his claim is a false one. More depends on his decision than his
own ambitious hopes. Is he to desert all those who have shared his
adventure and helped to sweep him on to success? Is he to abandon
the country—his country—to anarchy and civil war, now that Boris
Godunov is dead? The decision lies with him, and with him alone,
but both his character and the force of circumstances make it appear
predetermined: he cannot draw back. Here indeed is a situation
in which freedom and necessity are so intimately interlocked as to
become all but indistinguishable.

Demetrius chooses as he must, in the stress and strain of a crisis.
But, having thus chosen, he has to accept the consequences of his
choice as if that choice had been completely free. He has done
murder; he proceeds to usurp a throne; and the furies lie in wait
for him. Their work soon becomes apparent in the corruption of
his nature. Since he cannot believe in himself any more, he can no
longer bring himself to trust anybody. Whereas at the beginning
he appears as a young man of noble and lovable disposition—
proud, admittedly, and ambitious, but at the same time chivalrous,
capable of tenderness, generous and humane, we now witness a
sinister change in his temper and in his demeanour: he grows
moody, irritable, despotic, violent, and thus forfeits the affection
even of those who at first acclaimed him. It is a striking and subtle
instance of dramatic irony that the pseudo-Demetrius, having ousted
the other usurper, Boris Godunov, grows increasingly like the tyrant
whom he has supplanted, until he in his turn perishes as a victim of
rebellion.

Schiller's dramas have often been represented as the work of a
moralist. Gundolf, for example, asserts[2] that 'Schiller's drama is

---

[1] 'Säkular-Ausgabe' of Schiller's works, vol. 8, p. xxx.
[2] *Shakespeare und der deutsche Geist*, 6th edn., Berlin, 1922, p. 297.

founded, not (like Shakespeare's) on living entities, but on valuations; its basic principle is that the good and the bad fight it out, that right and wrong are balanced'. Without pausing to examine the full import of such a generalization, one may ask: how does it apply to *Demetrius*? Who are the 'good' characters in this play, and who are the 'bad'? In what sense are right and wrong balanced? Does the accession of Demetrius compensate for Boris Godunov's usurpation? In what sense can right be said to prevail at the end? Are the angry rebels who kill the hero to be regarded as instruments of ultimate justice, and does his death at their hands 'balance' his own wrongdoing?

Of course, it is possible to represent the fate of Demetrius as a judgment on his frailty; to say, quite simply, that he is punished for what he has done amiss, and to extract from the play the well-worn maxim that crime does not pay. But such a casting of moral accounts would hardly do justice to the work; it would trivialize a tragedy in which right and wrong are just as inextricably intervolved as freedom and necessity. It is true that in *Demetrius*, as elsewhere in Schiller's drama, we are made aware of the existence of a moral order, if by this we mean a divine pattern in the universe which is reflected in man's consciousness, in the *lex naturalis in corde scripta*. Behind and beyond the events of the play we sense the presence of a force that makes for righteousness. That force, however, works in mysterious ways, and its workings do not preclude the existence nor indeed the temporary triumph of evil. If it be true that 'the Lord will not suffer the soul of the righteous to famish,' there yet remains Job's bitter question: 'Wherefore do the wicked live, become old, yea, are mighty in power?' Schiller does not invoke the idea of an ultimate cosmic harmony in order to mitigate the harshness of tragic suffering. He does not make tragedy a handmaid of theology, and though he is painfully aware of the problem of the theodicy, he does not use his drama to propound a solution. Nor can Schiller's last play be profitably interpreted in the light of his own theory of the sublime. Demetrius is not the kind of protagonist who, recognizing his own guilt, reconciles himself (and us) to his tragic fate by a sacrificial and liberating act of self-surrender, like the heroine in *Maria Stuart* or like Don Cesar in *Die Braut von Messina*. Demetrius is not to be blamed for pursuing what he has good cause to regard as his legitimate aspirations; yet in so doing he creates the conditions which precipitate the crisis and lead to suffering and ruin. Like Wallenstein, he might say

> Wie anders! da des Mutes freier Trieb
> Zur kühnen Tat mich zog, die rauh gebietend
> Die Not jetzt, die Erhaltung von mir heischt.

When, more than half a century after Schiller's death, Hebbel decided to dramatize the story of the Russian pretender, he realized that there could be no question of starting where Schiller had left off. Goethe had tried to do that; he had meant to erect an enduring memorial to his friendship with Schiller by completing the fascinating fragment which his friend had left behind—and a famous passage in his *Tag- und Jahreshefte* for 1805 movingly records the sense of grief, of frustration, of irreparable loss which overwhelmed him when he found that he had to abandon the undertaking. Hebbel had no intention of renewing an attempt that was foredoomed to failure. 'Who could want to continue' (he wrote to Adolf Stern)[1] 'what the most subjective of all poets had begun?' Greatly though he admired Schiller's fragment, he soon came to the conclusion that he could not use a single line of it for his purpose. It is not hard to see why. Schiller's invention of a *fabricator doli* whose elaborate intrigue starts the hero on his career satisfied neither Hebbel's conception of historical drama nor his psychologizing turn of mind. In his view there had to be something more, and something more significant, behind the rise of Demetrius than a hired assassin's ingenious scheme of revenge. His hero, therefore, appears as the unwitting tool of the Jesuits, who hope to use the influence of a new czar in order to lead the Russian Orthodox Church back into the fold of Rome. As in Schiller's play, the crisis comes when the hero learns the truth about his origin. Unlike Schiller's Demetrius, however, Hebbel's is at once resolved to make the truth public and to withdraw from the scene; it is only for the sake of his supporters, and after much persuasion, that he agrees to go on acting the part which has been forced upon him. Nor is he guilty of murder, like Schiller's hero, or of any other crime. Tragic guilt, in Hebbel's sense of the term, need not involve any wrong-doing on the hero's part; it arises simply from the individual's self-assertion—'not, like Christian Original Sin, from the direction of the human will, but directly from the will itself'.[2] There is no need to show the hero, as Schiller does, with blood on his hands, and corrupted by power wrongfully exercised. The hero's

[1] October 31, 1858.   [2] *Mein Wort über das Drama.*

E

guilt in Hebbel's play is existential; it is of the fabric of his life. The ambiguity of his position is fully revealed when we learn the secret of his parentage, for in Hebbel's play Demetrius is a bastard son of Ivan the Terrible: not a legitimate claimant, as he had believed himself to be, but none the less the last descendant of the late Czar. The motif of illegitimacy, which Schiller had intended to use in his *Warbeck*, thus reappears in Hebbel's *Demetrius*.

Like Schiller's, Hebbel's *Demetrius* was left unfinished, though it was nearing completion. Whether it would have established itself in the repertory of the German theatre if Hebbel had lived to add the finishing touches is a matter of conjecture. It remains a fragment; and the spirit of the Russian pretender, unexorcised, continues to haunt the German stage.

V

THOMAS MANN AND SCHILLER

READERS of Thomas Mann are left in no doubt about the
literary and philosophical influences which helped to determine
his development and to shape his outlook. His indebtedness to
certain writers and thinkers is evident in all his writings, and this
debt of gratitude was handsomely repaid in the discerning studies
which he devoted to them. Nietzsche and Wagner, Schopenhauer
and Goethe are part of Thomas Mann's world—not merely as
purveyors of ideas or as sources of frequent and felicitous quotation,
but as a living presence. They are not just part of the furniture of his
mind; they are part of his inner life, and therefore of the substance of
his work. An incident in Nietzsche's life (the young student's
unintentional visit to a house of ill fame, his embarrassment and his
escape) is taken over, with slight modifications, into *Doktor Faustus*
and becomes a trigger-incident in the hero's career. The seduction
of Wagner's music (so brilliantly analysed in a number of Mann's
essays) loosens young Hanno Buddenbrook's tenuous hold on
life; Frau Klöterjahn succumbs to her illness after playing the
music of *Tristan*, in which the sweetness of passion blends with the
lure of death, and Wagner's use of the *leitmotiv* has its literary
counterpart in Thomas Mann's own style. As for Schopenhauer,
one remembers the chapter in *Buddenbrooks*[1] which shows the hero
deliriously carried away by *Die Welt als Wille und Vorstellung*:
how memorably it describes the impact of a philosophical system
on an untrained but susceptible mind! And can any biographer or
literary historian claim to have produced a more disturbingly
intimate portrait of the ageing Goethe than the author of *Lotte in
Weimar*? Mann's insight into Goethe's mind derives (as he himself
did not hesitate to point out[2]) from a sense of kinship, and certain
parallels readily suggest themselves. There is the same kind of home
background—literary genius cradled in a comfortable upper-
middle-class *milieu*; the same pride in patrician heritage and descent;
the same methodical and orderly conduct of life in the years of
maturity, the same consistent devotion to the daily task; the same

[1] Part 10, chap. v.
[2] Cf. the beginning of the essay 'Goethe als Repräsentant des bürgerlichen Zeitalters'; in
Adel des Geistes, 6th ed., Stockholm, 1948, pp. 104 f.

blend of playfulness with an underlying sense of mission and an almost preceptorial dignity; the same combination of bold long-term planning and careful management of resources.

Is Schiller to be counted among these literary household deities? At first blush one might be inclined to answer 'No'. If the average reader were asked to name Thomas Mann's literary and spiritual mentors, one may doubt whether the name of Schiller would spontaneously occur to him. Second thoughts, however, may lead to a rather different conclusion—a conclusion which the following pages are intended to establish.

It is true that Schiller figures less largely and less persistently in Thomas Mann's thought, and in the thoughts and experiences of his fictional characters, than Goethe or Wagner. Yet Schiller is too essential a part of Germany's literary heritage for any German writer to pass him by. It was thus not unnatural that Thomas Mann, the doyen of German letters, should have been invited to address those who forgathered at Stuttgart on the 150th anniversary of Schiller's death to do honour to the poet's memory—although (as he subsequently learnt from grateful and apologetic letters) some people had been doubtful about his qualifications for this task.[1] He acquitted himself admirably, having prepared his material with even more than his usual meticulousness: we know from his daughter's report what enormous trouble he took to distil the essence of his subject into the narrow space of his discourse.[2] Fortunately, the passages that had to be excised from the commemorative address were afterwards made available in the essay *Versuch über Schiller*.

Three months after the Stuttgart festivities, on August 12, 1955, Thomas Mann died. It so happens, therefore, that his essay on Schiller was his last offering to his readers and his last critical pronouncement. A mere coincidence, no doubt; but not, one feels, a wholly meaningless coincidence, nor in any way a paradoxical one. In penning his tribute to Schiller, Thomas Mann was re-traversing ground that had long been familiar. In 1905, the year of the centenary of Schiller's death, he had published a short sketch in which Schiller figured as the principal character. It shows the poet at work on his *Wallenstein*, and it depicts, in a few brilliantly evocative pages, one of those hours of discouragement and frustration which again and again delayed the completion of the formidable task. Hence its title: *Schwere Stunde*. In his essay of 1955, a con-

[1] Cf. Erika Mann, *Das letzte Jahr*, Frankfurt, 1956, p. 30.   [2] Ibid., pp. 12 f.

siderable part of which is devoted to *Wallenstein*, Thomas Mann again dwells on the situation of the poet wrestling with his recalcitrant material, chafing under his physical infirmities, weary, dejected, and at times despairing. These passages inevitably call forth echoes from the earlier study and so link up Thomas Mann's last work with its forerunner of half a century ago.

The Schiller study of 1905 has been much admired, and with good reason. It is a fascinating piece of writing, sensitively conceived and finely organized; from the very first sentence—an abrupt and deceptively casual opening—it brings Schiller to life, draws the reader into the orbit of his thought, and creates the mood of crisis. Slight though it is, it reveals more of the essential quality of Schiller's mind and character than many a full-length biography. What was it, one wonders, that enabled Thomas Mann to achieve, in so restricted a compass, such a compelling portrayal? What is it that gives this study its peculiar power and intensity?

The answer is not far to seek. *Schwere Stunde* portrays a poet whose works are not fed by a copious vein of inspiration but built up, bit by bit, by dint of persistent effort; a writer whose successes are won, and often narrowly won, by warding off the constant threat of failure; whose genius reveals itself in an infinite capacity for taking pains and for suffering pain; and who prevails, not by effortless facility but by vigilant self-criticism: a hero whose heroism takes the form of an unremitting struggle against his own weakness. We meet this type of hero again in one of Thomas Mann's most famous stories, *Der Tod in Venedig*. The principal character, Gustav Aschenbach (or *von* Aschenbach—for like Schiller he receives a patent of nobility in recognition of his merits) is a writer whose impressive achievements are the result of perseverance and self-discipline; he attains something like greatness by carefully husbanding his slender resources; he is the favourite author of all those—and they are many—who habitually drive themselves to the point of exhaustion and who succeed, by sheer force of moral determination, in carrying a burden that is too heavy for them. The affinity between Aschenbach and the hero of *Schwere Stunde* would have been obvious, even if Thomas Mann had not gone out of his way to direct the reader's attention to it. However, to make sure that the point will not be missed, he represents Aschenbach as the author of an eloquent and illuminating treatise on aesthetics which, as we are informed, is ranked by competent critics with Schiller's essay *Über naive und sentimentalische Dichtung*. It is equally obvious, on the other hand, that in some respects Aschenbach is unlike Schiller. When we read about his carefully ordered life, about his rigid timetable which reserves the best hours of the morning for his creative work, we realize at once that this does not tally with what we know of Schiller's habits. There are other differences. Aschenbach's parents are of different racial origin and social background. He marries a young lady whose family has some claim to academic distinction. He lives in circumstances of assured and solid comfort. All these traits do not fit Schiller: but they fit Thomas Mann. The same double resemblance appears in Aschenbach's writings. His critical treatise is explicitly likened to Schiller's famous essay; but other items in the list correspond unmistakably to Thomas Mann's own works—to *Buddenbrooks*, to *Tristan*, to *Fiorenza*, to *Königliche Hoheit*, to *Felix Krull*, and to the essay on Frederick the Great. On one occasion Thomas Mann purports to quote a characteristic remark from Aschenbach's writings. It expresses the conviction that all great achievements are acts of defiance—defiance of grief and pain, of poverty, loneliness, weakness, vice. This observation, we are told, embodies a personal experience; it is the formula of Aschenbach's life and fame, the key to his art. Aschenbach's art? The quotation, in fact, is from one of Thomas Mann's own essays, *Über den Alkohol*. It is thus 'inconspicuously tucked away in one of the author's less-known works', as he explains, with the air of the conscientious chronicler, when he ascribes it to the hero of his story; and the conviction imputed to Aschenbach is his own.

Aschenbach, then, is first cousin to the Schiller of *Schwere Stunde*, but at the same time, and no less plainly, his portrait is a self-portrait of Thomas Mann. May we not conclude that Mann himself must have felt in some way akin to Schiller? Indeed, it is only by virtue of such an affinity that he could have attained the insight which he displays in *Schwere Stunde*. He, too, belongs to that category of reflective writers whom Schiller contrasts with the 'naive' type of poet. Schiller's treatise had been a landmark in Thomas Mann's intellectual development; he continued to regard it as the most characteristic work of German literary theory—'the classical and comprehensive essay of the Germans, which includes all the rest and renders them superfluous'.[1] The author of *Schwere Stunde*, identifying himself with his hero, saw life and art through Schiller's

---

[1] Cf. the essay 'Goethe und Tolstoi', in *Adel des Geistes*, Stockholm, 1948, p. 182.

eyes; he was thus able to enter into the mixed feelings of admiration, love and envy which determined Schiller's attitude to Goethe. Step by step he traces the associations of ideas in Schiller's mind which lead, by an irresistible inner compulsion, to the thought of 'the other one', the serene and sensuous genius, divinely gifted, secure in his unassailable world.

Looking back on his life in old age, Thomas Mann, on his own admission, took pleasure in the order and symmetry of the pattern as he surveyed it in his mind's eye, in its coherence, its correspondences and cross-references. It seems fitting, therefore, that the picture of Goethe seen through the medium of Schiller's mind—inevitably a one-sided view—should have its counterpart in a picture of Schiller as he lived in Goethe's memory. Its lineaments emerge, almost a quarter of a century later, in the seventh chapter of *Lotte in Weimar*. The bulk of this lengthy novel (all except the short final chapter) deals with the events of two days, September 22 and 25, 1816: the day on which Charlotte Kestner—Werther's Lotte—arrives in Weimar and the day on which she has dinner at Goethe's house. By showing how the personality of the great man is mirrored in the minds and feelings of a variety of characters, Thomas Mann contrives to convey an astonishingly vivid impression of Goethe at the age of sixty-seven. In such a presentation the memory of Schiller had to find a place, for it was a memory ever present to his mind, and in any analysis of his mind that presence has to be reckoned with.

It makes itself felt, insistently and pervasively, in the *monologue intérieur* which takes up the greater part of chapter vii. This chapter —a striking example of parody born, not of malice, but of love— purports to let us listen in to the flow of thoughts that pass through Goethe's mind as he wakes up shortly before seven o'clock on the morning of September 22, 1816, and as he prepares to face the demands of a new day. In following the stream of his consciousness, with its ramifications and cross-currents, the associations, the reminiscences, the sudden flashes of illumination, the reader becomes aware of a recurring motif in the shifting pattern. Again and again the interior monologue turns into an imaginary duologue; a conversation with an unseen partner whose reactions Goethe tries to anticipate, whose approval he invites, whose criticism he seeks to forestall: and that partner is Schiller. A new literary project stirs in his mind: but who is there to spur him on, to encourage, and to provoke? No sooner has the question been asked

than the shade of Schiller appears on the imaginary scene, heralded
by a quotation from Goethe's own requiem for his departed friend:
'Wär Er noch da,

> der vor so manchen Jahren —
> Schon zehne sind's! — von uns sich weggekehrt!'

It had been a strange friendship, strange and precarious; a friendship sustained by the mutual attraction of opposites, full of personal
and intellectual tension; not without its undertones of irritation, and
indeed antipathy. Even in retrospect, a relationship of this kind
can hardly be viewed with detachment. Schiller had at one time
been a thorn in Goethe's flesh, and his memory remains a challenge.
'Did I ever like him?' Thomas Mann's Goethe asks himself (not
for the first time, one feels); 'did I ever like that proud invalid,
the aristocrat of the intellect, the champion of moral freedom,
the messiah who wanted to be a business man as well—always so
insufferably eager to assert himself, to prove that he had a right to a
place at my side. . . . Disagreeable schemer. Did I ever like him?
Never. Didn't like his stork-like gait, his red hair, his freckles, his
hectic cheeks, his round shoulders, his hook-nose never clear of
colds. And yet—what talent, what soaring courage, what a sure
sense of beauty, what facility of self-expression, what a superb
command of all his faculties, no matter how ill he felt. . . . I shall
not look upon his like again. To whom can I talk about *Faust*
now? He understood the difficulties, and the ways and means to
solve them. He smiled with pleasure when I read him the opening
of the Helena scenes. Oh yes, he had the seeing eye, and a sense of
humour to boot; a free, infinitely tolerant spirit—there was no
mistaking his distinction. . . .'

Reminiscences such as these are the medium through which we
see Schiller in Thomas Mann's novel. We see him as he is remembered by an imaginary Goethe whose feelings about him are un-
comfortably double-edged: admiration which may at any moment
turn into censure; affection which insists on keeping its object at
arm's length. What the reader is shown is not a straightforward
portrayal, but a reflection of a reflection in a mirror. Such a presentation could hardly have been intended to be Thomas Mann's last
word on the subject. It would have been a great pity if that last word
had remained unsaid, as it might have done, had not the Schiller
anniversary of 1955 provided the occasion before it was too late.
The *Versuch über Schiller* is dedicated to the poet's memory as a
labour of love: 'Seinem Andenken in Liebe gewidmet.' This

dedication, addressed to the tragedian by the humorist, is more than a pious gesture. It defines the author's approach to his subject, and it reminds the reader of what was lacking when he was being shown Schiller through Goethe's eyes. It may be over-optimistic to say, with Tennyson, that we needs must love the highest when we see it; it remains none the less true that it is only by loving it that we can hope to make it our own. As Schiller memorably expressed it in one of his letters on *Wilhelm Meister*:[1] 'Wie lebhaft habe ich bei dieser Gelegenheit erfahren . . ., dass es dem Vortrefflichen gegenüber keine Freiheit gibt als die Liebe.'

Thomas Mann's *Versuch über Schiller* is written with a literary artist's affection for the poet who had made the meaning and mission of art his principal theme; who had glorified it in words 'in which even the humblest of writers recognizes, with modest pride, his own suffering and his own joy'. The warmth of the author's feelings, however, does not cloud his judgment. He makes no attempt to gloss over the less endearing traits, but these traits are shown to be the defects of Schiller's great qualities. Although there are many touches of irony to enliven his portrayal, there is no malice. He notes the juvenile streak in Schiller, for instance, a naïve, boyish hankering after the sensational and the extreme; he refers to his interest in conspiracies and rebellions, in torture, intrigue, adventure, to the delight he takes in 'playing at Red Indians'; and he goes on to show how these foibles connect with that innate sense of the dramatic which gives Schiller's plays their lasting appeal. It was this irrepressible vitality that triumphed over all attempts to bowdlerize his first play. Thomas Mann pays tribute to it in an exciting passage. Having described the violent impact of *Die Räuber* on its first audience, he adds this comment:

'It becomes apparent that something deep within the play had resisted all attempts to alter it. "Go on", it said, "I defy you: do your worst." It had been impoverished, weakened ten times over, emasculated, disfigured, debased; but it stands out as an example of an immanent and inborn dynamic power which proved indestructible.'

In a sense, this triumph of his first play at its first performance was the most decisive event in Schiller's career. As time went on, other successes followed, less sensational perhaps than that first one, though hardly less resounding. There was, for example, the enthusiastic reception of *Die Jungfrau von Orleans* at its performance

[1] July 2, 1796.

in Leipzig. Thomas Mann describes it: the flourish of trumpets as the author leaves the theatre, the torches, the cheers; and Schiller passing through the waiting crowd, 'a little embarrassed, as usual, by this roaring success, which was not (as far as he knew) what he had been aiming at, and which was yet the object of his nature's deepest inborn urge'. Reading this description, one is reminded of various passages in which Thomas Mann voices similar feelings. One thinks, for instance, of the early autobiographical sketch *Im Spiegel*, in which he considers his career with ironical detachment and equally ironical disapproval. One recalls the half-embarrassed, deprecating note of his speech on his fiftieth birthday. Or one remembers a speech delivered at Yale[1] which contains the following remark:

'The artist who, thanks to involuntary achievements, begins to acquire a personal share in the supra-personal dignity of art, is instinctively and ironically on the defensive against what is called success, against the worldly honours and advantages of success'— an attitude (as he goes on to explain) which may very well be reconciled with ambitions of a different sort.

What is the explanation of this paradox of the artist whose in-most nature desires success, and who is nevertheless surprised and embarrassed when success comes his way? It is only natural for a writer to hope for public recognition; the reception accorded to his work can hardly be a matter of indifference to him. But to hope for recognition is one thing: to court popularity by pandering to the taste of the multitude is another. Neither Schiller nor Thomas Mann were concerned to give the public what the public wanted. They both sought to satisfy their own exacting standards, and there is nothing hypocritical about their sense of surprise when their readers were found to relish what they were being given, though it was not what they had been looking for, or what they thought they wanted.

Strangely enough, their single-minded devotion to their art drew upon both men the reproach of escapism. We are all too familiar with the aura of other-worldliness that surrounds Schiller in the works of some of his biographers. One remembers, too, the equally false picture drawn more recently by some Marxist critics—of Schiller the revolutionary *manqué*, the *bourgeois* who did not rise to the great challenge of the French Revolution because he could not

---

[1] 'Zur Gründung einer Dokumentensammlung in Yale University'; in the volume *Altes und Neues*, Frankfurt, 1953, p. 382.

bring himself to face up to the real issues of his age.[1] As for Thomas
Mann, no one could accuse him of having kept out of the dust and
heat of the political arena: his political speeches and pamphlets
would make nonsense of any such accusation. But he was charged
by German critics, both during and after the war, with having kept
callously aloof from the martyrdom of Germany; with having
watched the agony of his native land from a safe distance, uncom-
prehendingly; with having retired, in the comfort of his Californian
home, into the remote world of his novels while Germany was
enduring humiliation and defeat. Someone said about him, parody-
ing Goethe's famous dictum after the battle of Valmy, 'he can say
that he was not there'.

Thomas Mann answered these critics in the speech which he
made at Frankfurt in 1949. 'Not at all', he replies; 'I was there.
How can anyone who has read the sad story of Dr. Faustus maintain
that I was not there?' It is a dignified reply, and most readers of
Doktor Faustus will probably agree that it rings true. We hear the
same note of conviction when Thomas Mann defends Schiller
against critics who misrepresent his faith in art as a mere evasion of
unpalatable facts. Schiller knew more about the predicament and
the needs of modern man than the self-styled realists who would
meet those needs by political action or economic controls. He was
convinced that what is needed to save man from the threat of war
and self-destruction, and from the equally terrible danger that
lurks in the mechanization of life, is a change of heart. Social and
political progress, he holds, depends on the outlook and conduct of
individual men and women: and Thomas Mann urges his contemporaries to pay heed to Schiller's counsel when (in his Announce-
ment of *Die Horen*) he calls for 'the quiet building up of sounder
notions, clearer principles, and nobler morals, on which any
improvement of our social condition must in the last resort depend'.

How, in practice, is this desirable end to be attained? There can
be no simple answer; none but an ideological quack would venture
to prescribe a nostrum. But Schiller believed that poets and writers
could help, and Thomas Mann shared this belief. In his essay on
Chekhov (which preceded the Schiller essay), he writes:[2]

'To poor Katya's question [in Chekhov's *A Dreary Story*]: "What
am I to do?", one can only return the answer: "Upon my soul and

---

[1] For a criticism of these views, see W. Witte, *Schiller*, Oxford, 1949, pp. 61 ff., and 'Law
and the Social Order in Schiller's Thought', *infra*.
[2] *Nachlese*, Berlin and Frankfurt, 1956, p. 56.

honour, I don't know." And yet one works, one tells stories, one gives form to the truth, and thus entertains a needy world, in the obscure hope, almost in the confident belief, that truth and serene form may well liberate the soul and prepare the world for a better, a more beautiful, a more spiritual life.'

Here, translated into a different idiom and transposed, as it were, into a minor key, we have Schiller's idea of the 'aesthetic education of man'.

Schiller's reputation has had its ups and downs. There are those—and serious critics among them—who are inclined to write him off as a literary period piece, interesting but out of date. It looks, however, as if his detractors were unlikely to have the last word, for at present there are welcome signs of a revival of interest in Schiller. Thomas Mann contributed to a new assessment by demonstrating the significance of Schiller's work and thought in the world of to-day and its relevance to our troubled age. In doing so, he repaid the debt he owed to one whose influence on his own development, though less conspicuous than Goethe's or Wagner's, was yet far greater and deeper than it appears at first sight.

VI

LAW AND THE SOCIAL ORDER
IN SCHILLER'S THOUGHT

CRITICS who strive to re-write German literary history in terms of the class struggle represent Schiller as a revolutionary who stopped half-way, or less than half-way. 'Schiller is a *petit-bourgeois*, idealistic revolutionary ... whose ideological assault upon the Germany of feudal absolutism founders at an early stage, before the French Revolution.' The author of this judgment, Georg Lukács,[1] follows Mehring in maintaining that German literature towards the end of the eighteenth century and at the beginning of the nineteenth must be regarded as 'the ideological preparation of the bourgeois democratic revolution in Germany'. The real key to the friendship of Goethe and Schiller, for instance, is to be found in 'the fundamental economic and political views and aims' which they held in common;[2] both men, it is argued, sympathized to some extent with the desire for social reform which erupted in the French Revolution; both, however, rejected the 'revolutionary method', and especially its 'plebeian' character. This rejection cost Schiller dear, for it eliminated from the range of his subjects 'the deepest tragic problem of his era'[3]—i.e. the problem of modern capitalism—thus restricting the horizon of his drama to questions of private relationships, devoid of public significance.[4] To quote a characteristic comment—characteristic both as an expression of the author's attitude and as a sample of his style:[5]

> Er suchte nicht aus dem modernen Leben selbst jene Züge herauszuentwickeln, die in sich eine Öffentlichkeit enthalten, sondern versucht mit artistischen Mitteln ein künstliches Milieu zu schaffen, in dem das rein Private zum Öffentlichen idealistisch aufgebläht wird.

Both Goethe and Schiller, Lukács asserts, realized that the climate of modern capitalist society is hostile to art and literature;[6] both fought against 'the degradation of man by capitalist division of labour';[7] both strove to overcome 'the specific ugliness and the specifically inartistic character of bourgeois life'.[8] Occasionally Schiller seems to suspect that there might be a way of resolving

---

[1] Georg Lukács, *Goethe und seine Zeit* (Berne, 1947), p. 54.   [2] Ibid., p. 52.
[3] Ibid., p. 67.   [4] Ibid., pp. 87 f.   [5] Ibid., p. 88.
[6] Ibid., pp. 58, 77, 102.   [7] Ibid., pp. 81, 109.   [8] Ibid., p. 73.

the contradictions inherent in bourgeois society. But these are just vague inklings, confused and unformulated;[1] in general, his approach to the problem of reconciling reality with a humanist's creed remains incurably bourgeois, and therefore wrong-headed and ineffectual. His classicism, like Goethe's, seeks to ennoble middle-class life, imparting to it a monumental quality:[2]

> Diese Erneuerung der Antike geht deshalb in der Richtung der dichterischen Monumentalisierung des bürgerlichen Lebens.

He did not know (indeed, how could he?) that 'a historic-systematic dialectic of the development of art is possible only on a materialistic basis';[3] and since this insight had not been vouchsafed him, there remained only the way of the escapist—a flight into Utopian dreams of an intellectual and moral *élite*: 'an idealistic cul-de-sac'.[4] As another writer of similar persuasions puts it:[5]

> Dieser vom Volk losgelöste Idealismus, diese Flucht in die Aesthetik und dies Ausweichen ins Nur-Dichterische als Folge gesellschaftlicher Vereinsamung und politischer Rückständigkeit des Bürgertums brachten es mit sich, daß einer der fortschrittlichsten Geister der Epoche seine wortmächtige Kraft ins Fremde und Ferne lenkte.

This interpretation—whatever one may think of the philosophy on which it rests, or of the manner in which it is expressed—has, at all events, the merit of simplicity. But does it, perhaps, over-simplify matters? Schiller is sometimes wrongly represented as a poet and dramatist *manqué*;[6] is it any more justifiable to regard him as a revolutionary *manqué*? Before hazarding an answer, it might be as well to consider some of the evidence contained in Schiller's own writings. What do his works and his letters tell us about his attitude to social questions, and to the institution which forms the main support of any social order and which, at the same time, mirrors its character most accurately: the law?

> Das Gesetz [exclaims the rebellious hero of Schiller's first play] hat zum Schneckengang verdorben, was Adlerflug geworden wäre. Das Gesetz hat noch keinen großen Mann gebildet, aber die Freiheit brütet Kolosse und Extremitäten aus. (I, 2)

Here, and in his subsequent actions, Karl Moor appears as the advocate of anarchy. He is disgusted with a state of society that affords no remedy against the oppressor's wrong and the insolence

---

[1] Ibid., p. 108.   [2] Ibid., pp. 52, 56, 92.   [3] Ibid., p. 103.   [4] Ibid., p. 109.

[5] Gustav Leuteritz, in an article entitled 'Schiller oder das goldene Zeitalter', published in the (East) Berlin paper *Tägliche Rundschau* to commemorate the 190th anniversary of Schiller's birth on November 10, 1949.

[6] E.g. in M. Gerhard, *Schiller* (Berne, 1950); cf. the present writer's review in *M.L.R.* XLVI (January 1951), 129–30.

of office; a society in which the dead hand of convention stifles all healthy growth; in which the servile place-hunter flourishes, while worthy men fail to gain recognition, and sweated labour pays for the extravagance of irresponsible, pleasure-loving rulers. His decision to become a bandit, though precipitated by private disappointment, is intended partly as a protest against the injustice of a corrupt social order; he preys on the rich in order to solace some of the downtrodden poor. Before long, however, he realizes that the condition of society in general, and the lot of the underprivileged in particular, will not be improved by anarchy, and that mere lawlessness will not advance the cause of justice. One of his last speeches at the end of the play sums it all up:

> O über mich Narren, der ich wähnete, die Welt durch Greuel zu verschönern und die Gesetze durch Gesetzlosigkeit aufrecht zu halten! (v, 2)

What's done cannot be undone; but an act of atonement remains possible, and the great rebel recants, voluntarily submitting to the law which he had outraged:

> Aber noch blieb mir etwas übrig, womit ich die beleidigte Gesetze versöhnen und die mißhandelte Ordnung wiederum heilen kann. Sie bedarf eines Opfers, eines Opfers, das ihre unverletzbare Majestät vor der ganzen Menschheit entfaltet — dieses Opfer bin ich selbst.

A fictional character may, or may not, be the mouthpiece of the author's own views. In this instance, one need not hesitate to identify the author's opinions with his hero's, both at the beginning and at the end of Karl Moor's career of banditry. Schiller, who had been brought up in a society which attached much importance to class distinctions and privilege, and who had seen something of the misuse of absolute power (e.g. the arbitrary imprisonment of C. F. D. Schubart and J. J. Moser), clearly shared his hero's resentment. Indeed, as Professor Bruford reminds us, with explicit reference to four of Schiller's plays, 'to understand any work with a political bearing as it was understood then, we need always to remember that almost every German state was ruled by an autocrat'.[1] But although Schiller sympathizes, and invites his readers to sympathize, with Karl Moor's indignation, he takes care to repudiate his hero's actions. In the poem *Monument Moors des Räubers*, and in his prefaces to the play, he makes it quite clear that his work is not meant to be a glorification of violence. Karl Moor may be a quixotic kind of criminal, a criminal with a social conscience, and not without nobility: he remains a criminal none the less, an erring soul

---

[1] W. H. Bruford, *Germany in the Eighteenth Century* (Cambridge, 1935), pp. 20 f.

who in the end finds his way back: 'Der Verirrte tritt wieder in das Geleise der Gesetze', as the author puts it in his Preface to the first edition. The 'rejection of the revolutionary method' which Lukács notes in the writings of Schiller's maturity could hardly be expressed more plainly. Such being the conclusion of his very first play, it can hardly be maintained that in his later work Schiller went back on the revolutionary credo of his youth. It is worth noting that it is Spiegelberg, the most contemptible member of the band, who ironically expounds the 'beneficent' effects of the outlaws' assault upon society:

> Reichen Filzen ein Dritteil ihrer Sorgen vom Hals schaffen, . . . das stockende Geld in Umlauf bringen, das Gleichgewicht der Güter wiederherstellen, mit einem Wort, das goldne Alter wieder zurückrufen, dem lieben Gott von manchem lästigen Kostgänger helfen . . . — siehst du, das heiß ich ehrlich sein, das heiß ich ein würdiges Werkzeug in der Hand der Vorsehung abgeben. (I, 2)

In spite of the ending, however, and in spite of the author's protestations, it was the rebellious tone of the play, its social criticism, that captured the imagination of the contemporary public. The play was regarded, and has been regarded ever since, as an inspired indictment of a corrupt social system. No one could quarrel with that reading, or deny its relevance. But when critics speak of Schiller's 'ideological assault upon the Germany of feudal absolutism', it should be added, by way of qualification, that the assault is directed against the abuses of the system rather than against the system as such. Schiller denounces the villains and the parasites of the régime: the dissolute prince who ruins Kosinsky's happiness, and the servile courtier who panders to his lusts (III, 2); the venal official or the unscrupulous lawyer who makes a mockery of justice (II, 3); or the squire who ruthlessly exploits the peasantry (II, 3). In one of the most memorable scenes of the play, Franz Moor, an extreme example of a sadist in a position of feudal authority, experiences a foretaste of his well-deserved damnation. On the other hand, we gather that under a kindly master like the old Count the same system produced harmony and happiness:

> Mein Vater [says Franz] schuf sein Gebiet zu einem Familienzirkel um, saß liebreich lächelnd am Tor und grüßte sie Brüder und Kinder. (II, 2)

In a sense, such paternalism is (as Kant points out)[1] the most despotic kind of government imaginable; yet the rebel Karl confesses (IV, I)

---

[1] In the treatise entitled *Über den Gemeinspruch: Das mag in der Theorie richtig sein, taugt aber nicht für die Praxis*, sect. II.

that there was a time when he wished for nothing better than to follow in his father's footsteps:

Hier solltest du wandeln dereinst, ein großer, stattlicher, gepriesener Mann — hier! hier der Abgott deines Volks —

A similar conclusion may be drawn from *Fiesco*. In spite of its sub-title—'Ein republikanisches Trauerspiel'—the play in its original, authentic form does not sustain the theme of republican freedom; and the happy ending of the revised stage version, in which the ambitious leader of the conspiracy renounces his prize as soon as it is within his grasp, is too unconvincing to carry much weight. It is true that Gianettino Doria's pretensions meet with general resistance; he flouts the laws and the constitution, and his accession as Doge of Genoa would mean a reign of terror. It is true, too, that in a few speeches absolute rule is criticized as an institution, irrespective of the person of the ruler, because of its corrupting effect; in IV, 14, e.g.:

Selten stiegen Engel auf den Thron, seltner herunter . . . Fürsten, Fiesco? Diese mißratenen Projekte der wollenden und nicht könnenden Natur! Sitzen so gern zwischen Menschheit und Gottheit nieder — heillose Geschöpfe, schlechtere Schöpfer![1]

In the end, however, even Verrina, the most determined and high-principled of republicans, who does not shrink from killing Fiesco as soon as it becomes clear that his *coup d'état* was intended to satisfy a selfish ambition, is prepared to acknowledge the authority of the old Doge, Andreas. As in his poem *Die schlimmen Monarchen* from the *Anthologie auf das Jahr 1782*, the author of *Fiesco* censures wicked monarchs rather than the institution of monarchy. Fiesco's conspiracy, 'a picture of ambition in action, and ultimately defeated',[2] does not in any real sense aim at a reform of the social order. There is no question, for example, of curbing the privileges of the nobility, or of giving the common people a larger measure of political power; nor can the representatives of the lower orders whom we meet in II, 8 be said to qualify for any kind of self-government. It may not have been inappropriate for the French National Assembly to make Schiller an honorary citizen of the French Republic, which they did in 1792; but the reader of his 'republican tragedy' cannot fail to observe that 'M. Gille' wore his republicanism with a difference. When the diploma reached him, belatedly, in 1798, the difference had become more marked; the authors of the

---

[1] The same idea occurs in the *Briefe über Don Carlos*, Letter 9: ' . . . herausgetreten aus seiner Gattung, um als ein Mittelding von Geschöpf und Schöpfer — unser Mitleiden zu erregen.'
[2] Letter to Dalberg, November 16, 1782.

F

Xenien had made fun of the German partisans of the Revolution, suggesting that they adorn their red caps with bells, to complete the fool's garb:

> Lange werden wir euch noch ärgern und werden euch sagen:
> Rote Kappen, euch fehlt nur noch das Glöckchen zum Putz.

In *Kabale und Liebe*, Schiller's only tragedy of common life, the social criticism is more pointed, and more specific. It is directed against class prejudice and the evils of autocracy. The social conditions which form the background of *Die Räuber* are here depicted in concrete and painfully realistic detail. The common people have to pay for their sovereign's expensive amusements with their labour, and sometimes with their very lives. While they work hard to make a modest living, witless aristocrats like von Kalb fritter away their time in empty ceremonial, and careerists like von Walter jockey for position at court. The machinery of the law can be used for criminal purposes, as in III, 1, the scene in which von Walter and Wurm are planning to intimidate Miller and his family:

> Wir setzen also in aller Stille den Musikus fest — die Not umso dringender zu machen, könnte man auch die Mutter mitnehmen — sprechen von peinlicher Anklage, von Schafott, von ewiger Festung und machen den Brief der Tochter zur einzigen Bedingnis seiner Befreiung.

The nobility look down upon the middle classes with contempt. Even the heroine, with all her qualities of heart and mind, regards the barrier that separates her class from Ferdinand's as insuperable. She has been brought up to see in the social hierarchy of her time a universal, divinely appointed order which it would be sinful to transgress:

> Mein Anspruch war Kirchenraub . . . Laß mich . . . einem Bündnis entsagen, das die Fugen der Bürgerwelt auseinandertreiben und die allgemeine ewige Ordnung zugrund stürzen würde. (III, 4)

This sense of social inferiority has entered into her soul; it combines with her deep attachment to her father to paralyse her will and to wreck her life.

Being in more ways than one the most revolutionary of Schiller's plays, *Kabale und Liebe* is of special interest in the context of the present inquiry. What does it tell us about the author's outlook? Clearly, Schiller pities such victims of the social order as the old servant whose sons have been dragooned into 'volunteering' to go overseas and fight in the American War of Independence, or the paupers who are forced to work in the Duke's silver mines (II, 2);

his sympathy is with the under-privileged, including the middle classes. He would not be an artist, however, if he failed to aim at a proper distribution of light and shade: the representatives of the bourgeoisie in the play are not all virtuous, and the members of the ruling class are not uniformly wicked. Nor does the play suggest that the reform of the social system which is so obviously overdue will be initiated by those who have most to gain by it. Luise's submissive resignation is typical of the class to which she belongs— a class which does not think in terms of revolutionary action, or even of social evolution, but turns to religion for comfort in distress, hopes for justice on the Day of Judgment, and looks for equality in a life beyond the grave. 'Am jüngsten Gericht sind wir wieder da!' is the cry of the press-ganged soldiers as they depart for America (II, 2); and Luise speaks of a time when all class distinctions will vanish away, and men's worth will no longer depend on wealth or inherited titles:

> ... wenn die Schranken des Unterschieds einstürzen. ... Menschen nur Menschen sind ... der Vater hat ja so oft gesagt, daß der Schmuck und die prächtigen Titel wohlfeil werden, wenn Gott kommt, und die Herzen im Preise steigen. (I, 3)

The only two characters in the play who are prepared to oppose the established order are Lady Milford and Ferdinand, both aristocrats by birth, and both closely connected with the sovereign and the governing clique. In breaking with the Duke, Lady Milford makes it clear that her action is meant as a gesture of protest against persistent misrule; before she departs, she does what she can to alleviate the suffering of the poor (II, 2 and IV, 9). Ferdinand is determined to fly in the face of convention and prejudice by marrying Luise; he insists on their human rights and takes his stand on a universal natural law in resisting the misuse of power:

> Kann der Herzog Gesetze der Menschheit verdrehen oder Handlungen münzen wie seine Dreier? (II, 3)

It would appear, then, as if Schiller conceived of social progress, not as the result of a mass movement, sustained by the pressure of impersonal economic forces, but rather as the achievement of individual men and women who possess sufficient independence of mind to question the values and to criticize the mental habits of their own privileged class. Whether such a view deserves to be called 'revolutionary' depends on the precise meaning one attaches to that overworked adjective; it is probable, however, that the more radical kind of revolutionary would prefer to describe is as mildly reformist.

Turning to *Don Carlos*, one finds that reform, rather than revolution, is again the keynote. In his own commentary on the play, the *Briefe über Don Carlos*, Schiller insists (in the eighth Letter) that the dramatic interest centres on the two enthusiasts' project of bringing about 'the happiest conditions attainable to human society'. The main point in their programme—indeed, the only one that is made perfectly clear—is religious toleration, freedom of conscience, freedom of thought and inquiry. Apart from this one point, 'the daring vision of a future state' of which Posa speaks (IV, 21) is only vaguely adumbrated. It is to be a liberal state, which respects the rights of its citizens and makes their happiness its principal concern; a state in which, under the paternal guidance of an enlightened government, the individual's freedom of action is restricted only by the equal rights of his fellow-citizens (III, 10). Although Schiller speaks of 'republican virtues' (*Briefe über Don Carlos*, Letter 8), he makes it plain that this 'highest possible ideal of civic happiness' is to be realized under the beneficent rule of a prince. There is no question of overthrowing the monarchical form of government and the social order that goes with it. Improvement is to be attained, not by demolishing the existing political machinery, but by placing it under the control of a warm-hearted, high-minded, imaginative ruler.

In a conversation with Eckermann in which Schiller figured prominently (January 18, 1827), Goethe pointed out that the idea of freedom which runs through all Schiller's writings assumed a different aspect as Schiller himself changed with the advancing years. 'In his youth', Goethe continued, 'it was physical freedom that preoccupied him and entered into his works; in later life it was ideal freedom'. The statement is somewhat sweeping, and must not be pressed too far (it is not easy to see how it applies to *Wallenstein*, and to *Wilhelm Tell* it does not apply at all). Nevertheless, it is illuminating, for the inner freedom of the soul is indeed a recurrent theme in Schiller's later plays—notably in *Maria Stuart* and *Die Braut von Messina*—as well as in his philosophic treatises. In these works we are no longer dealing with rebels against society who want to change the world they live in; the emphasis is rather on man's ability to overcome the evils of this world, to rise superior even to disaster, by developing and disciplining his spiritual resources. Do these later tragedies, then, betoken a change of front?

Does Schiller, in thus modulating the theme of freedom to a spiritual key, abandon his former convictions, and disavow his 'revolutionary' past? Does he seek to conceal this *volte-face* (from himself, perhaps, as well as from others) by a flight into a non-committal aestheticism, divorced from real life? Is the phrase 'dies Ausweichen ins Nur-Dichterische' an apt description? By no means. 'The daring vision of a future state' of which Posa speaks in *Don Carlos* remains undimmed; in a sense it is more daring than ever. What has changed is not the aim, but the approach. The Jacobin Terror was providing the world with an object lesson in revolutionary technique. The lesson was not lost on Schiller, who was disgusted with the excesses of the Revolution.[1] His analysis of the matter is to be found in the *Briefe über die ästhetische Erziehung des Menschen*, as well as in some of his poems and historical essays. The cardinal point of his argument is a simple one: against the tyranny of mass movements and party programmes, Schiller vindicates the fundamental importance of the individual. The training of the individual personality, of mind, character, and taste, is a prerequisite of social and political advance. Without it, the overthrow of governments or the redistribution of incomes hold out slender hopes of success:

Alle Reform, die Bestand haben soll, muß von der Denkungsart ausgehen . . .[2]

or, as he puts it in the seventh Letter of the *Briefe über die ästhetische Erziehung*:

. . . bestätigt die Erfahrung mein Gemälde der Gegenwart, so muß man jeden Versuch einer solchen Staatsveränderung so lange für unzeitig und jede darauf gegründete Hoffnung so lange für schimärisch erklären, bis die Trennung in dem innern Menschen wieder aufgehoben und seine Natur vollständig genug entwickelt ist. . . .

Any state which becomes an end in itself and in which the individual citizen is no more than a cog in a machine is bad; the more efficient its administration, the greater the mischief. Sparta under Lycurgus serves Schiller as an example:

Der Staat selbst ist niemals Zweck [he writes in *Die Gesetzgebung des Lykurgus und Solon*, 1790], er ist nur wichtig als eine Bedingung, unter welcher der Zweck der Menschheit erfüllt werden kann, und dieser Zweck der Menschheit ist kein andrer als Ausbildung aller Kräfte des Menschen, Fortschreitung.

This harmonious development of the human personality, however, can take place only when the material basis of man's existence is assured. Schiller is well aware that it is cruelly disingenuous to

---

[1] Cf. his letter to G. Körner of February 8, 1793.
[2] Letter to Duke Friedrich Christian of Holstein-Augustenburg, July 13, 1793.

talk about the dignity of man so long as men are forced to live in conditions of degrading poverty. The distich *Würde des Menschen* puts the point succinctly:

> Nichts mehr davon, ich bitt euch. Zu essen gebt ihm, zu wohnen;
> Habt ihr die Blöße bedeckt, gibt sich die Würde von selbst.

The matter is argued more fully in one of his letters to Prince Friedrich Christian of Holstein-Augustenburg (November 11, 1793). It is the first duty of the state to look after the physical welfare of its subjects; not because material comfort is in itself a particularly worthy aim, but because so long as men have to exhaust their energies in the struggle for mere existence, no spiritual development, no 'aesthetic education', is possible.

> Erst muß der Geist vom Joch der Notwendigkeit losgespannt werden, ehe man ihn zur Vernunftfreiheit führen kann. . . . Wäre das physische Wohl nicht die Bedingung, unter welcher allein der Mensch zur Mündigkeit seines Geistes erwachen kann — um seiner selbst willen würde es bei weitem nicht so viel Aufmerksamkeit und Achtung verdienen. Der Mensch ist noch sehr wenig, wenn er warm wohnt und sich satt gegessen hat, aber er muß warm wohnen und satt zu essen haben, wenn sich die bessere Natur in ihm regen soll.

Compared with the strident note of his early plays, Schiller's tone has become more restrained; but restraint does not imply either the weary resignation of one who has given up hope, or the smugness of one who, having managed to feather his own nest, no longer cares about others; it merely shows that Schiller has come to understand the difficulties that face the social and political reformer. He diagnoses those difficulties as being primarily spiritual. It would not have occurred to Schiller to regard the achievements of the human mind and the objects of human faith as a mere superstructure, wholly determined by the economic basis on which it rests; on the other hand, he had not always found it easy to keep the wolf from the door, and was therefore not likely to ignore the material conditions of human existence, or to underrate their importance. Flight into aestheticism? The phrase does not fit. There is nothing evasive about Schiller, and those who do not like his answers should at least, in fairness, give him credit for having faced the questions.

Schiller's last play, *Wilhelm Tell*, depicts the revolt of the Swiss Forest Cantons against the rule of Albert I of Habsburg, who wants to reduce Switzerland to the status of an Austrian province: a struggle which (in the words of H. A. L. Fisher) 'marks the first triumph of the democratic principles in Europe over an area larger than the city state'.[1] The people's fight for political freedom cannot but affect the social order. A section of the Swiss aristocracy (represented in the play by Ulrich von Rudenz) is dazzled by the splendour of the imperial court, and more than half inclined to side with Habsburg against their own fellow-countrymen. The men who meet at the Rütli accordingly make no attempt to enlist the aid of the nobility, and prepare to act independently. Their self-reliance gives them a new dignity and a new confidence in their future. Political leadership is passing into other hands. In a dying vision Baron Attinghausen sees new life blossoming from the ruins of the old feudal order:

> Hat sich der Landmann solcher Tat verwogen
> Aus eignem Mittel, ohne Hülf der Edeln,
> Hat er der eignen Kraft so viel vertraut —
> Ja, dann bedarf es unserer nicht mehr,
> Getröstet können wir zu Grabe steigen,
> Es lebt nach uns — durch andre Kräfte will
> Das Herrliche der Menschheit sich erhalten.

When Rudenz, in the concluding line of the play, declares that all his bondsmen are henceforth to be free, one feels that he is merely anticipating the inevitable.

Spectacular though it is, however, this social landslide does not, and is not meant to, result in a dead level of equality. On the contrary, the representatives of the Swiss people whom we meet in the play are very conscious of their respective places in the social scale. There is a marked difference between a man like Stauffacher, who acknowledges no fealty save to the emperor, and those who (like Jost von Weiler) pay tribute to some lord of the manor. At the bottom of the scale, there are those who are in some sense *glebae adstricti*, owing personal service to a nobleman or to the Church, like the two men whom Melchthal introduces in the Rütli scene, and who are welcomed by Stauffacher, not without a touch of condescension:

> Gebt mir die Hand. Es preise sich, were keinem
> Mit seinem Leibe pflichtig ist auf Erden;
> Doch Redlichkeit gedeiht in jedem Stande.

They are allowed to take part in the deliberations of the assembly; but their civic rights are limited, for they are debarred from holding office:

> Kein eigner Mann kann Richter sein in Schwyz.

There is no question of abolishing these class distinctions, or of

[1] *A History of Europe* (London, 1938), pp. 342 f.

repudiating established obligations. The people rise in defence of their chartered rights, but their spokesmen make it clear that they have no wish to see innovation running riot:

> Die alten Rechte, wie wir sie ererbt
> Von unsern Vätern, wollen wir bewahren,
> Nicht ungezügelt nach dem Neuen greifen.
> Dem Kaiser bleibe, was des Kaisers ist;
> Wer einen Herrn hat, dien ihm pflichtgemäß.

Schiller depicts this display of moderation with obvious approval; like Stauffacher and Walther Fürst, he appears to hold the view that 'orders and degrees Jar not with liberty, but well consist'. As he put it some years earlier, in *Das Lied von der Glocke*, extolling 'sacred, blessed Order':

> Jeder freut sich seiner Stelle,
> Bietet dem Verächter Trutz.

In the peroration of his speech before the assembly—a justly famous passage—Stauffacher invokes the natural law to which men turn for justice when the normal proceedings open to them under the existing laws (in this case a petition addressed to the emperor) have failed to bring redress. The notion of a Natural Law which informs and, at the same time, transcends and overrides ordinary legislation had long been familiar to Schiller, and played its part in his thinking on social and political questions. It appears, for example, in *Die Gesetzgebung des Lykurgus und Solon*; a code of law, it is argued, which regards human beings as a means to an end, and not as an end in themselves, strikes at the foundations of natural law and morality. The expression 'the laws of nature' (in the sense of *ius naturale*) occurs in Schiller's translation of Louis-Sébastien Mercier's essay on Philip II of Spain (1786), and the same essay contains a sentence in which some lines from Stauffacher's speech are strikingly prefigured:

Sobald die Gesetze der Menschheit verletzt werden, tritt alles in das ursprüng-liche Recht zurück; einem unterdrückten Volke beizustehen und großmütig aufzuhelfen, das ist die Aufforderung der Natur;

> Wenn der Gedrückte nirgends Recht kann finden,
> Wenn unerträglich wird die Last — greift er
> Hinauf getrosten Mutes in den Himmel
> Und holt herunter seine ewgen Rechte . . .
> Der alte Urstand der Natur kehrt wieder,
> Wo Mensch dem Menschen gegenübersteht.

Schiller's attitude towards the doctrine of Natural Law brings his social and political philosophy into focus and defines his position.

Inasmuch as the doctrine sanctions criticism of positive law, it has revolutionary implications and may accordingly be put to revolutionary uses, as it was in Schiller's time—the time of the American and French Revolutions—when it re-emerged as a theory of natural rights. With some of these revolutionary implications Schiller was in sympathy. On the other hand, he saw, perhaps more clearly than some contemporary advocates of 'the rights of man', that the doctrine of Natural Law rests ultimately on a religious basis:[1] Stauffacher's phrase

> ... greift er
> Hinauf getrosten Mutes in den Himmel
> Und holt herunter seine ewgen Rechte

is no mere rhetorical flourish. Of the law of Moses (the Scriptural record of which forms an essential element of Natural Law as interpreted by the canonists),[2] Schiller remarks in *Die Sendung Moses*:

> Als ein Priester und Staatsmann aber weiß er, daß die stärkste und unentbehrlichste Stütze aller Verfassung Religion ist. ... Zur Gesetzgebung und zur Grundlage des Staats braucht er aber den wahren Gott, denn er ist ein großer und edler Mensch, der ein Werk, das dauern soll, nicht auf eine Lüge gründen kann.

The social reformer who takes his stand on the doctrine of Natural Law must accept its religious premisses; and in doing so, he parts company with all those who derive their programme of social reform from a purely materialistic philosophy.

Two conclusions emerge. First, Schiller's views on the social order and on law are more consistent than the contrast between the aggressive tone of his early plays and the restraint of his later writings might lead one to suppose. His early works are less 'revolutionary', and his later works less 'reactionary' (and less remote from practical experience), than they are often thought to be. In his mature writings, one is conscious of a change of tone, a tightening of artistic control; but there is no change of front, no betrayal of convictions. Something similar might be said about his private life. If, at Weimar and Jena, he came to terms with petty absolutism and aristocratic society, it was on his own terms that he did so.

---

[1] Cf. Cicero's classical formulation in *De Re Publica*, Lib. III, c. xxii (ed. by K. Ziegler, Leipzig, 1929): ' ... sed et omnes gentes et omni tempore una lex et sempiterna et inmutabilis continebit, unusque erit communis quasi magister et imperator omnium deus: ille legis huius inventor, disceptator, lator.'

[2] Cf. *Corpus Iuris Canonici* (ed. by E. Friedberg, 2nd ed., vol. I, Leipzig, 1879), Distinctio Prima: 'Ius naturae est, quod in lege et euangelio continetur.' Distinctio VII, c. i (De conditoribus legum): 'Moises gentis Hebreae primus omnium diuinas leges sacris literis explicauit.'

His ennoblement by imperial decree (in 1802) made no difference to him, as his comments show.[1]

Secondly, the criteria and categories of thought which critics like Lukács seek to apply to Schiller do not fit the case. That is why Lukács's analysis, though admirably knowledgeable and perceptive in many respects, remains, in the end, incongruous. When he dismisses Schiller as 'bourgeois', he uses an ideological label that does scant justice to the breadth of Schiller's thought and to his lack of class prejudice; and when he employs the word 'bürgerlich' in a Marxist sense, he arbitrarily detracts from its wider and fuller meaning, substituting the special terminology of historical materialism for common usage. Thomas Mann put the point admirably in his speech on *Lübeck als geistige Lebensform* (1926):

> The world revolution is a fact. To deny it would mean to deny life and development; to remain in obstinately conservative opposition to it would mean excluding oneself from life and development. But it is one thing to acknowledge the world revolution, and it is another thing to regard it, in all seriousness, as the annihilation of the German Bürger's way of life, and as a judgment on it. . . . A misleading over-emphasis is placed on questions of class and on economic matters. . . .

The statement applies to Weimar as it does to Lübeck. Where Schiller is concerned, this kind of bias produces criticism which, however agile intellectually, is apt to be deficient in sympathy, and therefore in insight.

[1] Cf. his letters to Cotta, November 27, 1802, and to Körner, November 29, 1802.

VII

GOETHE AND *IUS NATURALE*

IT was as a student of law that Goethe went up to the University of Leipzig in 1765; when, after his illness, he resumed his studies at Straßburg, he did so with a view to completing his legal training; and his student days ended in 1771 with the award of a law degree. All biographers duly record these facts: but few attach any great importance to them. While much space is invariably devoted to Goethe's affairs of the heart, to the influence of Merck and Herder, to his interest in folk poetry and Gothic architecture, to his reading of Shakespeare, and to his early dabbling in science, his study of law is usually dismissed with a few perfunctory remarks, as being of little or no account.[1] Hume Brown remarks of the young advocate that he had 'no interest in his nominal profession',[2] and this view recurs, with almost monotonous regularity, in other writers: in Henry W. Nevinson—'Law was too remote and abstract for a mind that depended almost entirely on sight and touch;'[3] in Georg Brandes—'Im tiefsten Innern aber lag die Jurisprudenz ihm wenig am Herzen';[4] in Emil Ludwig—'... denn inmitten allgemeinen Strebens muß seinem sinnlichen Geiste das theoretische Jus auch in Straßburg fremd bleiben';[5] in G. P. Gooch—'Goethe's heart was never in his profession';[6] in Professor Fairley, who declares that 'while he managed to become a lawyer of sorts, there can be no doubt that it all meant nothing to him and that it did nothing for him morally'.[7]

It has to be admitted that many of Goethe's own comments would seem to support this view. In *Dichtung und Wahrheit* (Part II, Book 6) he tells us how he arrived in Leipzig with the secret intention of substituting the study of languages, antiquities, and history for the course which his father had mapped out for him; how a

[1] A lengthy review article by Günther Müller shows that the subject is almost completely ignored in post-war Goethe criticism: cf. 'Goethe-Literatur seit 1945', *Deutsche Vierteljahrs-schrift für Literaturwissenschaft und Geistesgeschichte*, 1952, Nos. 1 and 3.
[2] P. Hume Brown, *Life of Goethe*, Vol. I, London, 1920, p. 81.
[3] Henry W. Nevinson, *Goethe: Man and Poet*, London, 1931, p. 28.
[4] Georg Brandes, *Goethe*, 4th ed., Berlin, 1922, p. 62.
[5] Emil Ludwig, *Goethe*, Vol. I, Berlin, 1926, p. 77.
[6] G. P. Gooch, 'Goethe's Political Background', *Studies in German History*, London, 1948, p. 168.
[7] Barker Fairley, *A Study of Goethe*, Oxford, 1948, p. 31.

somewhat uncomfortable interview with J. G. Böhme, the Professor of Jurisprudence, prevented that *volte-face*; and how, nevertheless, other pursuits soon took precedence of his legal studies. The same impression persists when we turn to those later chapters (Books 9, 10, and 11) which describe Goethe's sojourn at Straßburg. His work for his degree examination, done—after a fashion—in order to placate his father, is simplified by the services of a crammer; other interests predominate. Later on, as a practising lawyer in his native city, he let his father do the devilling for him, while the office routine was being taken care of by a competent clerk. At Wetzlar he saw something of the inefficiency and corruption of the court of appeal—a depressing spectacle, hardly likely to inspire a young lawyer with pride in his profession.

These retrospective comments in *Dichtung und Wahrheit* (as well as a few contemporary ones in similar vein)[1] cannot be lightly set aside. Nevertheless, the view in support of which they are cited remains inherently improbable. Goethe may have studied law against the grain; but he did learn enough to acquire his degree and to practise as a lawyer. Is it likely that this experience left no lasting mark? The evidence of his autobiography is perhaps less conclusive on this point than it may appear at first sight. *Dichtung und Wahrheit*, written when Goethe was in his sixties and seventies, is the story of the author's youth, seen in the perspective of advancing age; and a revealing sentence in Book 9 suggests that it does a little less than justice even to the Leipzig phase of Goethe's legal studies.

... mehr als ich in meiner bisherigen Darstellung aufzuführen Gelegenheit nahm, hatte ich bei meinem Aufenthalte in Leipzig an Einsicht in die Rechtserfordernisse gewonnen ...

In its almost casual way, this remark throws light upon an aspect of the matter which is usually ignored. Imagine a person of Goethe's quick susceptibility, of his intellectual grasp and his lively curiosity, coming into close contact, during some of the most formative years of his life, with one of the great creations of the human mind and with a supremely important institution: is it reasonable to acquiesce in the conclusion that it all meant nothing to him and did nothing for him? If it was a false start, must it therefore be assumed to have been completely fruitless? After referring to the

[1] Cf. the following letters: to his sister Cornelia, October 14, 1767 (*Der junge Goethe*, ed. M. Morris, Vol. I, Leipzig, 1909, p. 180); to Salzmann, December (?), 1771 (ibid., Vol. II, 1910, p. 119); to Kestner, September 15, 1773, and December 25, 1773 (ibid., Vol. III, pp. 54 and 73).

various occupations that attracted Goethe at different times—
drawing, science, statesmanship, theatre-management—Professor
Willoughby remarks:[1]

> If Goethe then goes on to describe these excursions as 'false tendencies', he does
> not mean that they could, or should, have been avoided. . . . Nor does he mean
> that they were in any sense unfruitful.

Are we to deny this principle of 'unity and continuity' where his
legal studies are concerned? One might as well argue that, because
at an early stage in his life Goethe ceased to be an orthodox Christian,
Christianity meant nothing to him—a point on which Thomas
Mann offers a vigorous comment:

> . . . it is *a priori* unthinkable (he writes)[2] that the fashioning of a spirit like his
> should not have been most strongly influenced by the most comprehensive
> revolution—or, rather, mutation—that the human conscience and world con-
> sciousness has ever experienced.

Günther Müller, in his *Kleine Goethebiographie*, sees the difficulty
and seeks to meet it. After some cursory references to Goethe's study
of law, he remarks:[3]

> Die spärliche berufliche Tätigkeit hat ihn nicht tiefer ergriffen. Immerhin wird
> sie an der Ausbildung seiner Denkformen wie an der Bereicherung seiner Vor-
> stellung vom Menschen mitgewirkt haben.

It is surely rather odd, however, that an influence which is admitted
to have enriched Goethe's conception of man and to have helped
to mould the cast of his mind should be dismissed in this cavalier
manner, in a sentence beginning with a deprecating 'immerhin'!

In his book, *Vom Wesen des Rechts in deutscher Dichtung*, Erik
Wolf has advanced the thesis that poets must have something to say
on the subject of law because law belongs to the essence of human
life.[4] If that applies, e.g., to Hölderlin, whose contacts with jurisprudence were of the slightest, how much more forcibly to Goethe,
who was trained to the law. He may not have cared for legal
technicalities. But in following his academic course—even the
rigidly utilitarian one prescribed at Straßburg—he could hardly
help reflecting on the underlying principles of law; and such reflections must have linked up, in the way which is so characteristic of
the working of his mind, with his thoughts on allied matters—on
nature, above all, and on the manifestation of the divine in the

---

[1] L. A. Willoughby, *Unity and Continuity in Goethe*, Oxford, 1947, p. 6.
[2] Thomas Mann, 'Goethe and Democracy', *Publications of the English Goethe Society*,
New Series, Vol. XX, 1951, p. 12.
[3] G. Müller, *Kleine Goethebiographie*, 2nd ed., Bonn, 1948, pp. 49 f.
[4] Erik Wolf, *Vom Wesen des Rechts in deutscher Dichtung*, Frankfurt a.M., 1946, p. 11.

natural order, one aspect of which is to be found in the concept of Natural Law.

There can be no doubt that the ancient doctrine of *ius naturale* loomed large in Goethe's legal studies. The schools of law in which he received his training had inherited their ideas from such distinguished teachers of natural law as Grotius, Pufendorf, Thomasius, and Christian Wolf.[1] Not that the interpretation of the doctrine remained constant. Its secular exponents in the age of rationalism would have rejected the view of the medieval canonists, who had laid it down that 'natural law is what is contained in Scripture and the Gospel';[2] and in the era of Rousseau, the era of the American and French Revolutions, the doctrine of natural law was transformed into a theory of natural rights. But although *ius naturale* did not mean in Goethe's day quite what it had meant in Roman and medieval times, and although it is hard to tell to what extent Goethe himself had pondered these changes of emphasis, it is certain that he was familiar with some aspects at least of the doctrine and of its history; for it appears, with an effect of deliberate paradox, in the first and the last of the *Positiones iuris* which he undertook to defend in his examination for the degree of Licentiate in Law. The first of these propositions is a definition of natural law, taken, almost verbatim,[3] from the *Corpus Iuris Civilis* and ascribed to Ulpian, a jurist of the third century A.D.: 'Ius naturae est, quod natura omnia animalia docuit.' The last (number 56), in claiming that slavery is founded in natural law, equates *ius naturale* with the 'law of nations' (*ius gentium*)—an interpretation which is not without precedent in Roman law.[4] Goethe relates in *Dichtung und Wahrheit* (Book 11) how he compiled the list of theses with the aid of his crammer. It may well be that the latter did the lion's share of the work; it may be, too, that Ulpian's questionable dictum in number 1 and the provocative assertion in number 56 were intended mainly as decorative flourishes at the beginning and at the end. Nevertheless it remains worth noting that Goethe chose to introduce and to

[1] Cf. Gertrud Schubart-Fikentscher, *Goethes Strassburger Thesen*, Weimar, 1949, pp. 13, 24 f., 28 ff.

[2] *Corpus Iuris Canonici* (ed. by E. Friedberg), 2nd ed., Vol. I, Leipzig, 1879. Distinctio Prima.

[3] Cf. *Corpus Iuris Civilis* (ed. by P. Krueger and Th. Mommsen), 6th ed., Vol. I, Berlin, 1893. The dictum 'Ius naturale est, quod natura omnia animalia docuit' occurs at the beginning of the *Institutiones* (Liber Primus, II) and of the *Digesta* (Liber Primus, I, 3).

[4] Cf. A. P. d'Entrèves, *Natural Law*, London, 1951, pp. 25 ff.; Heinrich Rommen, *Die ewige Wiederkehr des Naturrechts*, 2nd ed., Munich, 1947, p. 34; Gertrud Schubart-Fikentscher, *Goethes Strassburger Thesen*, Weimar, 1949, pp. 31 f.

conclude his theses with pronouncements on the subject of natural law.

The young licentiate, who presently applied to the authorities of his native city for permission to practise his profession as an advocate, was thus thoroughly familiar with the idea of a *lex naturalis in corde scripta*, which may have to be invoked against over-rigid positive enactments. Indeed, there was a school of legal thought which favoured such an appeal to common sense and natural feeling, as Goethe points out in *Dichtung und Wahrheit* (Book 13):

> Weil nun in jeder Zeitepoche alles zusammenhängt, so befolgte man in der Rechtslehre nunmehr auch nach und nach alle diejenigen Maximen, nach welchen man Religion und Moral behandelte. Unter den Sachwaltern als den jüngern, sodann unter den Richtern als den ältern verbreitete sich der Humanismus, und alles wetteiferte, auch in rechtlichen Verhältnissen höchst menschlich zu sein.

Goethe's very first case—Heckel *versus* Heckel—provides an illustration: in one of the lively memoranda which he addressed to the court in the name of his client,[1] he insisted

> ... daß die Handlungen der Menschen sich nicht nach steiffen Definitionen und Distinctionen fügen ...

What the student of law had assimilated remained embedded in the mind of the poet. To what extent did it enter into the poet's work? Influences of this kind cannot be isolated, and are therefore hard to assess. The conflict that may arise between the law in men's hearts and the law that is written in tables is a universal and recurrent motif: it appears in the *Antigone* as it does in *The Merchant of Venice*, in *Der Erbförster*, or in *Die Weber*. Obviously one does not have to study jurisprudence to become acquainted with it. And it may further be argued that in a revolutionary age no one could evade the challenge of the doctrine of natural human rights, as Goethe himself describes it in *Hermann und Dorothea*:

> Denn wer leugnet es wohl, daß hoch sich das Herz ihm erhoben,
> Ihm die freiere Brust mit reineren Pulsen geschlagen,
> Als sich der erste Glanz der neuen Sonne heranhob,
> Als man hörte vom Rechte der Menschen, das allen gemein sei ...

Undoubtedly, the idea of natural law, in the special sense of natural rights, was in the air. Still, the fact remains that Goethe's professional training directed his attention to its history and forced him to reflect on its meaning; and that fact can hardly be dismissed as insignificant. Where two forces work in the same direction, it may be difficult to decide how much either of them contributes to the

[1] Dated February 3, 1772; reprinted in Joh. Fuchs, *Advokat Goethe*, Weimar, 1932, pp. 63 ff.

total effect; but that does not mean that they do not both help to produce that total effect.[1] When someone who has qualified as a lawyer speaks of law and order, of justice, of innocence and guilt, the meaning of these words will for him be coloured by the discipline through which he has passed, even when they occur in a general, non-technical context. This view may be put to the test by considering some passages in Goethe's writings which invoke, either implicitly or explicitly, the idea of natural law.

Goethe frequently affirms his belief in a sense of law innate in man; he would have conceded universal validity to what St. Paul says of the Gentiles, 'which show the work of the law written in their hearts, their conscience also bearing witness' (*Romans* ii. 15). As he puts it in the poem *Vermächtnis*:

> Denn das selbstständige Gewissen
> Ist Sonne deinem Sittentag.

In a review of 1824,[2] he postulates an 'original virtue' in contrast with original sin:

> Wenn gewisse Erscheinungen an der menschlichen Natur uns nöthigen, ihr eine Art von radicalem Bösen, eine *Erbsünde* zuzuschreiben, so fordern andere Manifestationen derselben, ihr gleichfalls eine *Erbtugend*, eine angeborene Güte, Rechtlichkeit und besonders eine Neigung zur Ehrfurcht zuzugestehen.

Man's 'original virtue' is a reflection of that primal light of which he speaks in his *Vorspiel zu Eröffnung des Weimarischen Theaters* (1807); the light which, itself invisible, illumines the whole world:

> So im Kleinen ewig wie im Großen
> Wirkt Natur, wirkt Menschengeist, und beide
> Sind ein Abglanz jenes Urlichts droben,
> Das unsichtbar alle Welt erleuchtet.

All this, it may be noted, corresponds closely to the definition of natural law given by Thomas Aquinas:[3]

> It is as if the light of natural reason whereby we discern good from evil, which pertains to the natural law, were nothing but the imprint of the divine light on us. Hence it is clear that the natural law is nothing but the participation of the eternal law in the rational creature.

The examples quoted so far belong to the period of Goethe's maturity; but even before his departure from Frankfurt in the

---

[1] For a fuller statement of this argument, see W. Witte, 'The Sociological Approach to Literature', *Modern Language Review*, XXXVI, 1, January 1941.
[2] *Über Kunst und Altertum*, V, 1. The work under review is N. A. de Salvandy, *Don Alonzo ou l'Espagne.*
[3] *Summae Theologicae* Prima Secundae, Quaestio 91, Articulus ii; in J.-P. Migne's *Patrology*, 2nd series, vol. 2, Paris, 1841, column 701.

spring of 1770 he had entered the following observation in his *Ephemerides*:

> Getrennt von Gott und der Natur der Dinge zu sprechen, ist ebenso schwierig und bedenklich, wie wenn wir über Körper und Seele als etwas Getrenntes denken. Die Seele erkennen wir nur vermittels des Körpers, Gott nur durch die Natur.

This conviction, formulated in his student days, remained unshaken throughout his long life. An entry in his *Tag- und Jahreshefte* for 1811 refers to his

> angebornen und geübten Anschauungsweise, die mich Gott in der Natur, die Natur in Gott zu sehen unverbrüchlich gelehrt hatte;

which in turn reminds us of the well-known lines in the poem *Prœmion*:

> Was wär' ein Gott, der nur von außen stieße,
> Im Kreis das All am Finger laufen ließe?
> Ihm ziemt's, die Welt im Innern zu bewegen,
> Natur in sich, sich in Natur zu hegen . . .

That 'nature' in these contexts includes human nature is shown by Goethe's comment on a remark of Kepler's:

> Kepler sagte: 'Mein höchster Wunsch ist, den Gott, den ich im Äußern überall finde, auch innerlich, innerhalb meiner, gleichermaßen gewahr zu werden.' Der edle Mann fühlte sich nicht bewußt, daß eben in dem Augenblicke das Göttliche in ihm mit dem Göttlichen des Universums in genauester Verbindung stand.

The influence of such beliefs on men's moral conduct is stressed in the Notes to the *Westöstlicher Divan*, in the passage dealing with the religion of the Parsees:

> Eine so zarte Religion, gegründet auf die Allgegenwart Gottes in seinen Werken der Sinnenwelt, muß einen eignen Einfluß auf die Sitten ausüben.

It is obvious that all these pronouncements on a divine pattern in the universe which is reflected in man's moral consciousness are open to all the objections that have been raised against the doctrine of natural law. It has been argued, and with much force, that while the idea of natural law may appear inspiring at first sight, closer scrutiny shows it to be deplorably vague and unhelpful when applied to concrete cases. Men's moral intuitions, it is pointed out, their views on what is 'naturally' right, are by no means uniform; they depend on a man's upbringing, on his racial and religious affiliations, on his social background, and on his political convictions; they vary with time and circumstance. That applies even to matters which the medieval canonists singled out as falling within the purview of natural law, such as the relations between the sexes—'viri et feminae coniunctio'—, the rearing of children—'liberorum

G

successio et educatio'—, legitimate self-defence—'violentiae per vim repulsio'—, or the restitution of property held in trust—'depositae rei vel commendatae pecuniae restitutio.'[1] Examples are not far to seek. In the days of the patriarchs, polygamy was considered unexceptionable, as it is in some countries to-day; in Christian communities it is felt to be wrong. So is polyandry, which is the accepted social pattern in some societies. In ancient Greece, the exposure of children was in certain circumstances regarded as a right and proper procedure, whereas our feelings rebel against the deliberate killing of a defenceless infant. A convinced pacifist will deny the possibility of any 'righteous war', and a communist will show scant respect for a wealthy shareholder's right to cash in on his investments. Faced with such divergent opinions on fundamental issues, the legal positivist may well ask: what are we to make of the concept of natural law as Cicero defines it, in a passage which writers on this topic are fond of quoting—'a law which is the same as true reason, accordant with nature, universally recognized, constant and eternal'?[2] And what is the use of a theory that breaks down as soon as one tries to apply it to a definite case? As Sir Alexander Gray puts it, in his entertaining way:[3]

Without in any way speaking disrespectfully of Natural Law, its obvious weakness as a guide to everyday life is that it is so singularly silent on the Isle of Wight bee disease, the muzzling of dogs, and the precise day in October on which the close season for trout should begin.

And yet, however telling some of the positivists' arguments may be, there remains the conviction—not universal, admittedly, but certainly widespread—that they do not quite settle the issue. We may describe law as a record of national custom and social convention, as the consensus of a body of legislators, as the decree of political authority or as an expression of the will of the people; but only the most uncompromising materialist can content himself with a definition that takes no account of the idea of justice. True, laws may be unjust, and yet retain their compulsive force; and, as Goethe points out in one of his apophthegms, even an unjust law may well be preferable to lawlessness:

Es ist besser, es geschehe dir unrecht, als die Welt sei ohne Gesetz.

But it is equally true that such laws are felt to betray the ideal

---

[1] *Corpus Iuris Canonici* (ed. E. Friedberg), 2nd ed., Vol. I, Leipzig, 1879. C. vii: Quid sit ius naturale.
[2] Cicero, *De Re Publica* (ed. by K. Ziegler, Leipzig, 1915); Lib. III, c. xxii, 33: 'est quidem vera lex recta ratio, naturae congruens, diffusa in omnis, constans sempiterna. . . .'
[3] Alexander Gray, *The Socialist Tradition*, London, 1946, p. 130.

towards which all law must aspire without ever completely attaining it. That ideal is in essence religious; it derives from the faith in a divine world order. Our positive laws, Goethe held, are merely groping attempts to advance some way towards such an order, empirical approximations:[1]

Alle Gesetze sind Versuche, sich den Absichten der moralischen Weltordnung im Welt- und Lebenslaufe zu nähern.

When seen in this light, the positive law is often found wanting. In *Götz von Berlichingen*, e.g., the administration of justice is shown to be sluggish, ineffectual, and corrupt. When Götz, in the scene of the village wedding, encourages the peasants to protest against malpractice and to seek redress, he takes his stand (whether he knows it or not) on a principle of natural law which concedes validity to any legal ruling only in so far as it operates justly. The principle was formulated by Thomas Aquinas, who quotes St. Augustine in support:[2]

Augustine says: 'No law is valid unless it be just'; hence its legal force is in proportion to its justice. Now in human affairs we call a thing just when it is right according to the rule of reason: and the first rule of reason is the natural law.

Although, in another scene of the same play, the learned jurist Olearius extols the excellence of the Roman law, the arch-criminal Adelheid is in the end brought to book by an irregular secret tribunal—the Vehmgericht—which takes it upon itself to act where the regular courts have failed. It has no official constitutional standing, but it represents the common man's innate sense of justice, and its findings are prompted by that 'natural instinct' of which the *Corpus Iuris Canonici* speaks in its definition of natural law.[3]

The appeal to a universal law, more venerable and more compelling than national code or local custom, is heard again in *Iphigenie*, where it gains special significance from the context; for it is voiced by the heroine at the moment of supreme crisis when she stakes her own and her brother's fate upon her faith in such a law—a law (in Cicero's resounding phrase) 'which will not be different in Rome from what it is at Athens, nor different in the future from what it is now, but will remain valid for all nations and at all times, one, abiding, unchangeable'.[4]

---

[1] *Maximen und Reflexionen*, Weimar ed., Vol. XLII, ii, p. 215.
[2] *Summa Theologica*, ed. cit.; Prima Secundae, quae. 95, art. 2.
[3] *Corpus Iuris Canonici*, ed. cit., c. vii.
[4] Cicero, *De Re Publica*, ed. cit., Lib. III, c. xxii, 33: '. . . nec erit alia lex Romae alia Athenis, alia nunc alia posthac, sed et omnes gentes et omni tempore una lex et sempiterna et inmutabilis continebit . . .'

> Du glaubst, es höre
> Der rohe Skythe, der Barbar, die Stimme
> Der Wahrheit und der Menschlichkeit, die Atreus,
> Der Grieche, nicht vernahm?

asks Thoas, and Iphigenie replies:

> Es hört sie jeder,
> Geboren unter jedem Himmel, dem
> Des Lebens Quelle durch den Busen rein
> Und ungehindert fließt.

Putting her trust in what may be called a principle of natural law, she triumphs over subterfuge, distrust, and violence.

The character of Iphigenie reflects Goethe's faith in the inherent nobility of womanhood and in its redemptive virtue—that faith which is so memorably expressed in the concluding passages of *Faust*. It is true, of course, that some of Goethe's women characters—Klärchen, Cäcilie, Philine, Gretchen—transgress social conventions; but when it is a question of ultimate right and wrong, as distinct from mere conventional propriety, most of them are guided unerringly by the still small voice that speaks in their hearts.

> Ganz leise spricht ein Gott in unsrer Brust,
> Ganz leise, ganz vernehmlich, zeigt uns an,
> Was zu ergreifen ist und was zu fliehn

says the Princess in *Tasso* (III, 2). Therese in *Wilhelm Meister* echoes those sentiments:

> ... wem sein Herz nicht sagt, was er sich und andern schuldig ist, der wird es wohl schwerlich aus Büchern erfahren ... (Book 7, ch. 6).

So does the heroine's governess in *Die natürliche Tochter*:

> Und so verleugnet ihr das Göttlichste,
> Wenn euch des Herzens Winke nichts bedeuten.
> (II, 1, 862 f.)

Eugenie herself proves an apt interpreter of the natural law; in her first conversation with the young judge, she criticizes positive laws and legal institutions, as well as the officers of the law, for being unable to prevent the arbitrary use of autocratic power:

> Was ist Gesetz und Ordnung? Können sie
> Der Unschuld Kindertage nicht beschützen?
> Wer seid denn ihr, die ihr mit leerem Stolz
> Durchs Recht Gewalt zu bänd'gen euch berühmt?
> (IV, 2, 2005 ff.)

A state of affairs in which the general corruption of the body politic stultifies the law is described by the Chancellor in the second part of *Faust*. When the speaker laments the atrophy of 'that sense which alone can lead us to the Right' (ll. 4801 f.), he is manifestly thinking in terms of natural law—i.e. of a law that embodies, as one of its fundamental tenets, the injunction of the gospel, 'All things whatsoever ye would that men should do to you, do ye even so to them' (*St. Matthew* vii. 12), and which opposes that principle to a system where 'lawlessness rules by law': 'Wo . . . das Ungesetz gesetzlich überwaltet.'

In *Faust* I, elements of natural law doctrine appear when Mephistopheles, in his role as a temporary director of studies, advises the young student on the subject of jurisprudence. Mephisto sympathizes with the young man's reluctance to embark upon the study of law; he criticizes the inherent inertia of positive law, its failure to adapt itself to changing conditions, which tends to render it ineffective and oppressive. Unlike the bulk of the scene in which it occurs, the passage in question (ll. 1970–79) does not belong to the *Urfaust*; it was added a good many years later, in 1790. Written at a time when the political events in France were engrossing everyone's attention, it places the emphasis on rights rather than obligations. It is one of the ironies of the situation that Mephisto, in the guise of an elderly don, should be pandering to the revolutionary sentiments of the younger generation.

Such sentiments, needless to say, may be misguided; the name of natural law may be taken in vain to justify a purely subjective and irresponsible judgment on legal issues. Special pleading of this sort, if admitted, must undermine public confidence in the law and lead to mere anarchy. A case in point occurs in *Werther*. Carried away by compassion for a suffering human being whose fate mirrors his own, the hero seeks to secure the release of the young farm servant who has killed his rival, and when his eloquent plea is rejected, he tries to persuade the magistrate to let the prisoner escape. Werther, less clear-sighted than Gretchen, confuses the judgment of God with the course of justice on earth. It would be presumptuous for man to set any limit to the grace of God, who in His mercy may forgive even a murderer: Gretchen's penitent soul is admitted to the divine presence of the Virgin. But Gretchen, untutored though she be as compared with Werther, scorns the opportunity of evading the punishment which the law exacts. Werther's defence of homicide has no support in a natural law that includes the commandment 'Thou shalt do no murder'.

The theory of natural law has been criticized (as we have noted before) on the ground that it moves in the clouds and fails to come to grips with concrete reality. Positive law has to provide those detailed and explicit directives which are required when one is dealing with specific situations, such as a case of trespass or a third-party insurance claim, and the more precisely it formulates them the better. It must be remembered, however, that no regulations, however elaborate, can ever cover the infinite variety of human problems, and that a law is not necessarily useless because it lacks such regulative detail.[1] The decalogue, in its stark simplicity, affords some apt illustrations. In practice, as everyone knows, each one of the commandments raises a host of exceedingly difficult questions of interpretation. An injunction such as 'Honour thy father and thy mother', unequivocal though it may sound, becomes problematic as soon as one tries to translate it into definite rules of conduct. And yet, paradoxically, such injunctions may afford guidance where the more detailed ordinances of positive law are of no avail. That is what happens in *Die Wahlverwandtschaften*, a story that may be said to hinge on the meaning of the seventh commandment. A person whose marriage has broken down and who has become attached to someone else may well feel dissatisfied with the laws that govern contracts of marriage. Such feelings are voiced by the Count in the tenth chapter of Part I. He enlivens the company's table talk with tales of a friend who likes to air his theories about law reform in the sphere of marriage and divorce; but as soon as the would-be reformer's suggestions are mentioned, they are at once seen to be unacceptable. As far as the principal characters are concerned, the reader gathers that, under the existing laws of church and state, Eduard and Charlotte could obtain a divorce, and thus allow their elective affinities free play. But after the death of their child—the child who was conceived in such peculiar circumstances, and whose death is felt to be a judgment on Eduard's and Ottilie's contemplated union—Ottilie bows to the authority of a law which her action proclaims to be valid, although no earthly judge could enforce it.

The doctrine of natural law affirms the essential connexion between law and ethics. Law, it insists, is not merely the decree of sovereign power—'*ius quia iussum*': it has an inward authority, in proportion as it is just—'*ius quia iustum*'. It is clear, however, that this authority compels only men of good will; the wicked (as Cicero

---

[1] Goethe was well aware of this much-debated problem, as some of his Straßburg theses show: cf. Nos. 44, 50, 51, and Getrud Schubart-Fikentscher, *Goethes Strassburger Thesen*, Weimar, 1949, pp. 42 ff., 49 f.

points out in the passage previously referred to)[1] will neither recognize nor respect it. Fortunately, it is no part of the present argument to consider the logical difficulties that arise when natural law is described as a set of injunctions which are understood and obeyed by good men, and a good man as one who understands and obeys the injunctions of the natural law. (One may perhaps note, in passing, that if God is acknowledged as the ultimate source of all values and as the author of the natural law, the vicious circle disappears.) What is worth stressing in this context is the affinity between, on the one hand, the man who 'shows the works of the law written in his heart, his conscience also bearing witness', and, on the other hand, the kind of person whom Shaftesbury called a 'virtuoso', and whom German writers in the eighteenth century styled a 'schöne Seele'. Not that the two are identical. What distinguishes the 'virtuoso' is that his inclinations harmonize with his moral intuitions. Such a happy balance is rare; many a man (even a good and honourable man like Honorio in Goethe's *Novelle*), while in no doubt about the demands of the natural law, has to conquer himself before he can meet them. But while there is no question of identity, there is noticeable affinity. In both cases, intuitive insight reveals the right; and in both cases the law is felt to work from within, through the heart of man, not by any threat of external sanctions.

When asked how morality had come into the world, Goethe is reported by Eckerman to have said:

> Durch Gott selber, wie alles andere Gute. Es ist kein Product menschlicher Reflection, sondern es ist angeschaffene und angeborene schöne Natur. (April 1, 1827.)

We find this conception embodied in Wilhelm Meister's Natalie, of whom her brother Lothario says:

> Unerreichbar wird immer die Handlungsweise bleiben, welche die Natur dieser schönen Seele vorgeschrieben hat.
>
> (8th Book, ch. 10)

In one of the stories in *Unterhaltungen deutscher Ausgewanderten*, the young hero, Ferdinand, seeing the error of his ways, gradually discovers for himself a fundamental principle of natural law:

> Es ward ihm nach und nach deutlich, daß nur Treue und Glauben die Menschen schätzenswert mache, daß der Gute eigentlich leben müsse, um alle Gesetze zu beschämen, indem ein anderer sie entweder umgehen oder zu seinem Vorteil gebrauchen mag.

[1] Cicero, loc. cit.: 'vera lex . . ., quae tamen neque probos frustra iubet aut vetat, nec improbos iubendo aut vetando movet.'

Critics have pointed out that Goethe thought of law, as he did of nature, in terms of evolution. Law, like other human institutions, varies with varying conditions; it is the legislator's task to adapt it to the needs of his time.[1] How does this evolutionary conception fit in with the theory of natural law, which claims that certain principles of law are valid for all men, everywhere and at all times? The answer is that there is, in fact, no incompatibility; far from being mutually exclusive, the two views are really interdependent. If Goethe thought it desirable that the law should not be allowed to stagnate, that it should remain capable of growth and change, that does not mean that he approved of drifting with the tide of events. It is precisely in times of revolution, when laws are challenged and when legislators are all too apt to be swayed by the veering winds of political doctrine, that natural law comes into its own, for it serves as a beacon by which the wise reformer can set his course. In this matter, as in others, Goethe's thought was spacious enough to accommodate an apparent paradox and to make it fruitful. The influence of natural law theories on his views and his ways of thinking and, on the other hand, his evolutionary conception of law, may indeed be cited as an example of that polarity which he observed everywhere and which determined the cast of his own mind.

[1] Cf. Hans Fehr, *Das Recht in der Dichtung*, Berne, n.d. (1931), p. 422; Oswald Marcuse 'Goethe als Rechtsbildner', *Jahrbuch der Goethe-Gesellschaft*, Vol. IX, Weimar, 1922, pp. 5 f.

VIII

CARLYLE AS A CRITIC OF GERMAN LITERATURE

WHEN the hero of *Sartor Resartus* has won through to the revelation of the Everlasting Yea, after 'that high moment in the *Rue de l'Enfer*', he says to his own tormented self: 'Close thy Byron; open thy Goethe.' This injunction is of central significance; in a sense it is the formula of the book. Teufelsdröckh's victory in his battle against the terrors of the Everlasting No marks a turning-point in his creator's own development; in making his hero choose Goethe as his guide, Carlyle stresses an indebtedness to the master-spirit of German literature which he never ceased to acknowledge. Much critical light has since been thrown on the problem of German influence on Carlyle as a thinker and as a writer; and while the precise extent of this influence remains difficult to assess—for one must remember that as a rule an influence from outside only helps to bring out what the person concerned has it in him to be, and that the seed cannot germinate unless it lights upon the right kind of soil—its great importance for the formation of Carlyle's mind is universally admitted.

Nor can there be any doubt about his being the chief herald, in this country, of the literary revival that had just taken place in Germany. Others before him, it is true, had made more or less sustained efforts to familiarize the British reading public with some samples from the store of German literature. As early as 1796, Scott had published his translations of Bürger's *Lenore* and *Der wilde Jäger*, soon to be followed by his translation of *Götz*. In 1798–99, when Carlyle was scarcely out of his cradle, Coleridge had been in Germany and had met at least one of the leading lights in contemporary German letters, Klopstock—a meeting of which he left us such an entertainingly malicious account in *Biographia Literaria*. Disappointing as his contacts with the 'German Milton' may have been, Coleridge's stay in Germany bore fruit; soon after his return to England he published his magnificent translation of Schiller's *Piccolomini* and *Wallensteins Tod*. And had not Byron dedicated two of his tragedies to Goethe, in the most flattering terms, as 'the homage of a literary vassal to his liege lord, the first of existing writers'? On a more pedestrian level, William Taylor of Norwich had been busily at work for many years translating and introducing German authors, and in 1830 he had gathered these miscellaneous writings together in three volumes, under the title *Historic Survey of German Poetry*. This compilation was examined by Carlyle, searchingly and unsparingly, in the *Edinburgh Review*, and dismissed as inaccurate, undiscriminating, ill-informed— indeed, as 'one great Error'.[1] Carlyle's review demonstrates that as a student of contemporary German literature he had left even the best informed among his fellow-countrymen far behind. In a remarkably short time he had become an authority on a subject into which his predecessors had merely made a few haphazard incursions. 'Man', observes the Editor of Teufelsdröckh's strange writings, 'is emphatically a Proselytizing creature'. Carlyle was anxious to convert others to his newly-found faith, and his eagerness to share his revelation brought its own reward: in interpreting German literature, and more especially Goethe, to his fellow-countrymen, Carlyle found himself; his growth as a man and as a writer is mirrored in his characterizations of German authors and their works. These analyses are therefore of interest both as documents of Carlyle's biography and as a spectacular advance in the development of German studies in Britain. Focusing his attention on these aspects, the reader of to-day might almost be tempted to overlook or to underrate the value of Carlyle's pronouncements on German literature as literary criticism pure and simple. Yet their importance in that respect remains considerable and deserves to be reaffirmed.

With few exceptions,[2] the writings that fall to be considered in this context belong to the early phase in Carlyle's career which preceded his removal to London in 1834. His first substantial work, the *Life of Schiller*, was published serially in the *London Magazine* in 1823–24 and reissued in book form in 1825. All the remaining reviews and essays on German literature were products of the Craigenputtock years; they appeared in the *Edinburgh* and in its younger contemporaries—the *Foreign Quarterly Review*, the *Westminster*, the *Foreign Review*, and *Fraser's Magazine*. Thus Carlyle's criticism of German literature was produced during a period in his life which was still re-echoing with the sinister challenge of the

---

[1] Cf., however, Leslie Stephen's charitable summing-up in his essay on 'The Importation of German', *Studies of a Biographer*, Vol. II, London, 1910, pp. 65 ff.

[2] Viz., the article on 'Varnhagen von Ense's Memoirs' (*London and Westminster Review*, 1838) and the *Lectures on the History of Literature*.

Everlasting No; a time of mental stress and ferment that reached its literary consummation in *Sartor*. Carlyle-Teufelsdröckh had experienced his spiritual rebirth, and 'begun to be a man'; but although 'the old inward Satanic School' was conquered, it was by no means silenced; on the contrary, 'its howl-chantings, Ernulphus-cursings, and rebellious gnashings of teeth might, in the mean while, become only the more tumultuous. . . .' It was 'in the mean while' that Carlyle extended his knowledge of German literature, a first contact with Goethe having helped to precipitate the inward crisis; and who can blame him if his criticism, written as he proceeded with his German reading, sometimes reflects the agitation of these richly formative but troubled years?

Having acquired a working knowledge of German (originally for the purpose of reading a German book on mineralogy), Carlyle arranged for some books to be sent to him from Germany. Among the first eagerly awaited consignment of 'really German books' were the works of Schiller. More than forty years later he wrote: 'I well remember the arrival of the *Schiller Werke* sheets at Mainhill (and my impatience till the Annan Bookbinder had done with them) . . .'

It is not to be wondered at that Carlyle, with the shadow of the great crisis still upon him, should have been profoundly impressed by Schiller's steadfast and courageous devotion to an ideal. Here was a superb example of a dedicated life, a life with 'a noble inward unity'; here is a man who 'loves true spiritual Beauty with his whole heart and his whole soul; and for the attainment, for the pursuit of this, is prepared to make all sacrifices'. It was the moral quality of the man that interested and inspired Carlyle: in his early *Life of Schiller*, as in the Schiller essay of 1831, we find in his approach to literature that firm moral emphasis which was the keynote of his criticism. 'The Ideal Man that lay within him', he writes,[1] 'the image of himself as he *should* be, was formed upon a strict and curious standard; and to reach this constantly approached and constantly receding emblem of perfection, was the unwearied effort of his life'. (One remembers Schiller's trenchant dictum in his review of Bürger's poems: 'All that the poet can give us is his individuality. That individuality must therefore be worth exhibiting to the world and to posterity.') From the beginning Carlyle thus manifests what was to remain his strength as well as his limitation as a literary critic: his interest in the person of the author rather than in his work. He

[1] *The Life of Friedrich Schiller*, London, 1888, p. 40.

often displays remarkably keen insight as well as broad human sympathy in analysing an author's moral character; his portraits of literary men are for the most part drawn with an artist's touch, vigorous and lively, yet delicate when the occasion demands it; and when some trait in a writer strikes a chord in his own heart, he can rise to heights of memorable eloquence, as he does, for instance, in the concluding pages of his *Life of Schiller*. On more than one occasion, the reader of these earlier writings can see the doctrine of hero-worship casting its shadows before.

Goethe quickly recognized this tendency in the man who was proud to avow himself the aged poet's disciple. In a brief comment on the *Life of Schiller*[1] he speaks admiringly of Carlyle's insight into Schiller's character and excellent qualities, of his reverent and affectionate approach to his subject, and of his success in keeping 'the idea of an outstanding man' steadily in view. The German translation of Carlyle's book which appeared in 1830 was graced with an introduction from Goethe's pen,[2] written in similar vein. After recalling with pleasure how the author in his distant Dumfriesshire home had been stirred and moved by Schiller's writings and how they had stimulated him to pursue his studies in German literature, Goethe continues: 'I, at any rate, was touched to see how, even in those early works of our departed friend which were often harsh and almost crude, this stranger's calm, clear thought always perceived the noble, well-meaning, benevolent personality, and how in him he was able to create for himself an ideal of human excellence'; which is why he commends the *Life of Schiller* to the younger generation in particular, for it is the privilege and the duty of youth 'to see, even in what is not exemplary, the general exemplar of humanity'. Goethe sounded the same note in his conversations with Eckermann. 'It deserves admiration', he remarked (July 25, 1827), 'that in judging our German authors Carlyle is specially concerned with the intellectual and moral core, i.e. the essential active principle'. And he added, with prophetic intuition: 'Carlyle is a moral force of great importance.' Unerringly Goethe defines the nature of Carlyle's criticism and indicates its immanent trend: away from considerations of literary art, towards ethical and political issues. Other critics have since developed Goethe's pregnant remark,

---

[1] *Über Kunst und Altertum*, Vol. 6, 2.

[2] Goethe also supplied the publisher, Heinrich Wilmans, with sketches of Craigenputtock for the frontispiece and the title-page, and with drawings of Schiller's house at Weimar and of his summer house at Jena for the front and back covers. Cf. Paul Raabe, 'Ein Beitrag Goethes zur Weltliteratur,' *Imprimatur*, Vol. XII, Munich, 1954–55, pp. 181 ff.

analysing in greater detail Carlyle's characteristic insistence on the moral rather than the literary aspect of his subjects.[1]

There is no denying that this attitude, admirable, no doubt, in its own way, tended at times to impair Carlyle's judgment as a critic of literature. Why, for example, does he mar an otherwise stimulating appreciation of Schiller's *Die Räuber* by calling Amalia 'a beautiful creation', though she 'has few mortal lineaments'? Why does he express admiration for Leonore in *Fiesco*? Can it be that because these characters represent (however unconvincingly) an ideal of womanhood (however invalid), Carlyle failed to see how wooden and insipid they are? Again, why does he wax eloquent on the subject of Ferdinand and Luise in *Kabale und Liebe*, and at the same time dismiss all the other characters in a single inadequate paragraph, without so much as mentioning Schiller's memorable portrayal of Luise's father? Did he not realize that in doing so, he was conveying a false impression of the quality and texture of the play? Why does he dwell so lovingly on the figures of Max and Thekla in *Wallenstein*? Is it not because these characters, high-minded and gentle, help to provide the moral emphasis which he desired? From the premiss (correct enough in itself) that characters such as these were dear to Schiller's heart, Carlyle seems to have jumped to the unwarrantable conclusion that Schiller could not have felt any sympathy at all for a figure like King Philip in *Don Carlos*. He is thus forced to assert that 'in delineating Philip, Schiller seems as if struggling against the current of his nature', and that our feelings towards him 'are hardly so severe as he intended'. Moreover, he does his best to substitute a character Schiller is alleged to have had in mind for the one he really drew, with the result that Schiller's Philip, subtle, complex, brooding, and tragic, appears crudely simplified as 'the stony-hearted Despot'.

But if the moral perspective caused some distortion in his *Life of Schiller*, there is, on the other hand, enough sound and illuminating criticism in the book to warrant Saintsbury's opinion that 'it brands the author as a great critic *if he chose*'. But, as the same writer hastens to add, 'he did not wholly choose; and, later, he refused'.[2] In his last pronouncements on specifically literary matters, his London *Lectures on the History of Literature*, the refusal is definite. The moralist has ousted the critic. This is clearly seen, for example,

[1] F. W. Roe, *Thomas Carlyle as a Critic of Literature*, New York, 1910, pp. 40, 71, 101, and *passim*; Louis Cazamian, *Carlyle*, Paris, 1913, pp. 46, 84, 87; Jean-Marie Carré, *Goethe en Angleterre*, Paris, 1920, pp. 183 f.

[2] George Saintsbury, *A History of Criticism*, Vol. III, Edinburgh and London, 1904, p. 496.

in the passages dealing with Luther. We are given an admirable portrait of the mighty reformer, dauntlessly championing liberty of conscience; about Luther the writer, one of the giants of German letters, these lectures tell us nothing whatever, apart from a sadly perfunctory reference to his translation of the Bible.

Where little or nothing is known about an author's life, Carlyle cannot indulge his ethical-biographical leanings to the same extent, but must perforce concentrate on the text. His essay on the *Nibelungenlied* benefited by this kind of restriction; his comments (some of them in intuitive accord with the findings of subsequent research) everywhere bespeak his critical powers. Above all, he clearly recognizes the artistic unity of the work, its 'internal coherence and completeness'; and he gives full credit to the unknown poet who brought forth poetic order from the chaos of conflicting popular tradition and earlier redactions. The ancient sources of the poem, dating back to the times of the Migrations, had undergone various changes and accreted new elements during the intervening centuries: it was no easy matter to fuse these disparate materials into an organized whole. Yet the Austrian minstrel who, in the early years of the thirteenth century, produced the epic as we now have it, was equal to the task. With sure critical instinct Carlyle acclaims him as a true and great poet, vigorous yet sensitive, with an unconscious felicity of expression, an eye for character, and the epic poet's ability to marshal the figures and incidents of a long and intricate story.

Some errors, both in matters of fact and of judgment, are to be expected in the work of a pioneer. Few students of the poem would care to support Carlyle's assertion that the *Nibelungenlied* 'is what it professes to be, a *Song*'; nor can he be said to have given his readers an adequate account of the metrical pattern when he described the Nibelungen stanza as running on 'in more or less regular Alexandrines'. The full and accurate précis of the poem, on the other hand, might be described as a model performance if it were not for a certain patronizing archness which frequently obtrudes itself, a mock *naïveté*, mildly entertaining at times, but a little tiresome in the long run. His comments on the events on King Gunther's wedding night might be cited as an example. Gunther suffers the most ignominious treatment at the hands of his unrelenting bride and has to appeal to Siegfried for help; a situation which, while certainly not without its humorous aspects, leads straight to bitter tragedy. The following passage illustrates Carlyle's manner:

> Brunhild hints plainly that, unless the truth be told her, unpleasant consequences may follow. Thus is there ever a ravelled thread in the web of life! But for this little cloud of spleen, these bridal feasts had been all bright and balmy as the month of June. Unluckily too, the cloud is an electric one; spreads itself in time into a general earthquake; nay that very night becomes a thunder-storm, or tornado, unparalleled we may hope in the annals of connubial happiness.

The free indulgence of this whimsical vein fostered the rapid growth of Carlyle's prose style. Almost wholly absent in his *Life of Schiller*, 'Carlylese' can be seen blossoming forth in the Essays. To what extent German models contributed to its development remains a moot question; but there can be no doubt that when he describes Jean Paul's mode of writing, Carlyle is at the same time characterizing his own. That is what gives his description its special piquancy: his analysis is written in the style which he is analysing—'so fantastic, many-coloured, far-grasping, everyway perplexed and extraordinary . . .':

> Not that he is ignorant of grammar, or disdains the sciences of spelling and parsing; but he exercises both in a certain latitudinarian spirit; deals with astonishing liberality in parentheses, dashes, and subsidiary clauses; invents hundreds of new words, alters old ones, or, by hyphen, chains and pairs and packs them together into most jarring combination; in short, produces sentences of the most heterogeneous, lumbering, interminable kind. Figures without limit; indeed the whole is one tissue of metaphors, and similes, and allusions to all the provinces of Earth, Sea, and Air; interlaced with epigrammatic breaks, vehement bursts, or sardonic turns, interjections, quips, puns, and even oaths! A perfect Indian jungle it seems; a boundless, unparalleled imbroglio.

This similarity between Carlyle and Jean Paul is not merely a matter of coining odd words or taking liberties with conventional syntax; it also appears in the quality of imagination and invention that distinguishes their works. An example may serve to illustrate this. Jean Paul repeatedly shows himself averse to calling a chapter a chapter: in *Hesperus*, the sub-divisions of the book are designated 'Hundsposttage', because fresh material for further instalments of his novel is periodically brought to the author by a dog; in *Leben des Quintus Fixlein, aus 15 Zettelkästen gezogen*, the contents of the boxes of slips referred to in the title are supposed to determine the arrangement of the narrative. These whimsicalities have their counterpart in *Sartor*, where the biographical data, so urgently needed by the harassed 'Editor' of Teufelsdröckh's *magnum opus*, are eventually sent to him in 'six considerable PAPER-BAGS, carefully sealed, and marked successively, in gilt China-ink, with the symbols of the six southern Zodiacal Signs, beginning at Libra; in the inside of which sealed Bags lie miscellaneous masses of Sheets, and oftener Shreds and Snips, written in Professor Teufelsdröckh's scarce-legible *cursiv-schrift*; and treating of all imaginable things under the Zodiac and above it . . .'; and where we watch the poor Editor trying (or professing to try) to bring some semblance of order out of this German chaos, 'gathering, clutching, piecing the Why to the far-distant Wherefore', as he grapples with *Scorpio, Sagittarius, Capricornus*, and the rest.

When Carlyle seeks to justify Richter's manner as the self-expression of original if wayward genius, when he insists that 'there is no uniform of excellence, either in physical or spiritual Nature: all *genuine* things are what they ought to be', it is plain that he is, by implication, pleading his own cause. His plea is based upon the principles of that New Criticism which was, in Germany as elsewhere, challenging the preceptive Neo-classic methods; principles which Carlyle summed up so brilliantly, and with such warm approval, in *The State of German Literature*. Perhaps the most essential feature of the new critical doctrine is its catholicity: in Carlyle's own words, 'It is, indeed, the most sacred article of this creed to preach and practise universal tolerance'. Accordingly he holds that a curious literary phenomenon like Richter should not be judged by reference to any rigid system of rules, but on its own peculiar merits and 'by the event'. It is true that this latitudinarian attitude is still in some degree qualified by a demand for 'beneficent results'; but it is a far cry from the spirit of these essays, liberal, sympathetic, charitable, to the intransigence of their author's later years.

The Carlyle who maintains that 'the great law of culture is: Let each become all that he was created capable of being' thereby proclaims himself a convert to the faith which impelled Goethe to go on, unhasting yet unresting, rearing the mighty 'pyramid of his existence.'[1] The conversion, however, was not a permanent one, and some of Carlyle's critics endeavour to prove that it was at no time complete. One of them argues that in his study of German literature Carlyle was searching not for a new philosophy of life, but merely for confirmation of the moral convictions implanted in him by his Calvinist upbringing, and that, so far from being a convert to a new

---

[1] This highly characteristic expression occurs in a letter of Goethe's to J. K. Lavater, September (20th?), 1780.

Humanism, he was all the time trying—subconsciously if not consciously—to vindicate 'the creed of Ecclefechan'.[1] With special reference to Goethe, another writer points out that Carlyle tended to ignore the worldly, sensuous, pagan elements in the poet's nature, whereas he over-emphasized the idea of Renunciation.[2] No doubt there is some truth in these observations. Still, for a time Carlyle succumbed to the potent spell of genius; for a time something of the Master's serene humanity informed the temporary disciple's own writings; and his fervent admiration of the great poet, 'the Teacher and exemplar of his age', made him give of his best when he was writing about Goethe.

Not that the manner of his approach changes: it remains unequivocally that of the biographer and the practical moralist. He makes it clear that 'we are here looking at the work chiefly as a document for the writer's history'. He chooses to discuss Goethe 'chiefly as a world-changer, and benignant spiritual revolutionist', and insists that he deserves 'deep, grateful study, observance, imitation, as a Moralist and Philosopher'—although in another context he warns his readers (and with good cause) 'that this noble man, in respect of his heart, and goodness and badness, is not altogether easy to get acquainted with'.[3]

The reader who turns to Carlyle's essays on Goethe in search of literary appreciation thus may not quite find what he bargained for. Nevertheless he is not likely to be disappointed. Through the rich deposits of biography and moral reflection there runs a vein of criticism, thin, it is true, but of high quality, and well worth the quarrying. The spiritual crisis through which he himself had passed fitted Carlyle to understand *Werther*; his own *Sartor Resartus* reflects 'that nameless Unrest, the blind struggle of a soul in bondage'. True, the hero of *Sartor* (like Faust) is saved from suicide by the memory of his childhood faith; but for a long time his life, like Werther's, seems unendurable, and when he recalls his misery, his description of it paraphrases a passage from *Werther*. 'I lived', writes Teufelsdröckh, 'in a continual, indefinite, pining fear . . .;

---

[1] Cf. C. F. Harrold, *Carlyle and German Thought: 1819–1834*, New Haven and London, 1934, pp. 7 and 69 f.

[2] J.-M. Carré, loc. cit., pp. 144, 158, 178.

[3] Unfortunately the author of a popular text-book chose to ignore Carlyle's warning: cf. George Sampson's chapter on Carlyle in his *Concise Cambridge History of English Literature*, Cambridge, 1941, p. 696. A comparison with the corresponding chapter (by J. G. Robertson) in the large-scale *Cambridge History of English Literature* (Vol. XIII, Cambridge, 1916, pp. 6–7) shows that in this instance the author exercised to the full what he describes in his Preface (p. xii) as the epitomist's right to introduce 'certain modifications' of the views set forth in the parent work.

H

it seemed as if all things in the Heavens above and the Earth beneath would hurt me; as if the Heavens and the Earth were but boundless Jaws of a devouring Monster, wherein I, palpitating, waited to be devoured'. Werther had been through it all before Teufelsdröckh was thought of: 'Und so taumle ich beängstigt, Himmel und Erde und ihre webenden Kräfte um mich her: ich sehe nichts, als ein ewig verschlingendes, ewig wiederkäuendes Ungeheuer.' (Letter of August 18th.)

Did Carlyle recognize that *Werther* was something more than the voice of one particular generation, something more than a perfect expression of contemporary *taedium vitae*? One could wish that he had been a little more explicit on that point. He saw, however, that after the contagious fever of the *Werther* period had burnt itself out, Goethe was faced with the difficult task of prescribing a remedy for 'that high, sad, longing Discontent'. *Wilhelm Meister* was Goethe's answer—a satisfactory one, in Carlyle's view: 'the problem which had been stated in *Werther*, with despair of its solution, is here solved'. The transition from *Werther* to *Wilhelm Meister* is the transition from the denial to the affirmation of life and its duties, from the Everlasting No to the Everlasting Yea. It is wholly fitting, therefore, that after his conversion to a new faith in life, Teufelsdröckh should take his cue from *Wilhelm Meister*. He quotes Lothario's remark (as repeated by Jarno in Book 7, chapter 3 of *Wilhelm Meisters Lehrjahre*) 'Hier oder nirgend ist Amerika!' and the chapter on 'The Everlasting Yea' ends, characteristically, with two sentences in which scriptural and Goethean echoes blend: 'Whatsoever thy hand findeth to do, do it with thy whole might' (Cf. *Ecclesiastes* ix. 10). 'Work while it is called To-day; for the Night cometh wherein no man can work.' This calls to mind two lines from Goethe's *Westöstlicher Diwan*:

> Noch ist es Tag, da rühre sich der Mann,
> Die Nacht tritt ein, wo niemand wirken kann

which in turn derive from a passage in the Gospel according to St. John (ix. 4): 'I must work the works of him that sent me, while it is day: the night cometh, when no man can work.'

Occasional errors of judgment do not seriously impair the solid merits of these Goethe studies. One may be surprised to find Carlyle classing *Die Mitschuldigen*, that product of undergraduate cynicism, with works like *Werther* and *Götz* as belonging 'to the same dark wayward mood'; just as one cannot help wincing when, in his attractive essay on *Goethe's Helena*, he refers to the lines spoken by Lynceus as 'doggrel'. But such lapses are amply redeemed by frequent flashes of critical insight and verbal felicity, such as the passage in which he describes *Dichtung und Wahrheit* as revealing 'the . . . complex Possibility offered from without, yet along with it the deep never-failing Force from within'; or his analysis of Goethe's 'singularly emblematic intellect; his perpetual tendency to transform into *shape*, into *life*, the opinion, the feeling that may dwell in him'; or the account he gives, in his Translator's Preface, of the manifold beauties to be found in *Wilhelm Meister*. No doubt some of Carlyle's readers would gladly give up many pages of bio-graphical analysis if in exchange they could have critical discussions of such works as *Egmont* or *Die Wahlverwandtschaften*. But where so much has been done, it would be ungrateful to complain because more has not been attempted.

'What nobler work', asks the Editor of Teufelsdröckh's papers, 'than transplanting foreign Thought into the barren domestic soil?' Noble work it remains, even where the domestic soil is far from barren. Carlyle's *Life of Schiller*, his translations of Goethe's *Wilhelm Meister* and of stories by J. K. A. Musäus, Jean Paul, Ludwig Tieck, E. T. A. Hoffmann, Friedrich de la Motte Fouqué, as well as his articles on Novalis, Grillparzer, Zacharias Werner, and Adolf Müllner provided Goethe with a welcome opportunity of ventilating one of his favourite topics, the idea of world literature. 'National literature', he remarked in conversation with Eckermann (January 31, 1827) 'does not mean much nowadays; the epoch of world literature is due, and everyone must now endeavour to hasten its coming'. A few months later (July 18, 1827), when Eckermann had been reading Carlyle's essay on Fouqué in *German Romance*, Goethe paid tribute to the soundness of Carlyle's literary judgment and went on to say: 'It is very nice, though, that the close contacts between the French, the English, and the Germans now enable us to correct each other. That is the great advantage which accrues from a world literature . . .' In a letter to Carlyle written two days later, on July 20, 1827 (parts of which were subsequently incorporated in the comments on *German Romance* published in *Über Kunst und Altertum*, vol. 6), he develops these notions at some little length:

It is clear that the efforts of the best poets and creative writers of all nations have for some considerable time been directed towards what is common to all mankind. . . . And whatever in the literatures of all nations promotes and points towards this end is precisely the part which others must make their own. We must familiarize ourselves with the peculiarities of other nations in order to respect them, indeed in order to make them the very means of intercourse; for the peculiarities of a nation are like its language and its coinage: they facilitate intercourse—in fact, it is only through them that intercourse becomes fully possible. A truly universal tolerance will most surely be attained if we refrain from interfering with the peculiarities of individuals and peoples, at the same time holding fast to the conviction that the hall-mark of true merit consists in its belonging to humanity as a whole.

This was grist to Carlyle's mill. Anything that could help to breach the literary and intellectual barriers between nations, and between Britain and Germany in particular, was welcome; even an unsatisfactory book like William Taylor's *Historic Survey of German Poetry* might do some good. Having performed—more in sorrow than in anger, but with merciless efficiency—the 'all-too sordid but not unnecessary task' of tearing Taylor's book to shreds, Carlyle offers a crumb of comfort to the author and to those who had paid good money for his three volumes: 'Does not the existence of such a book, do not many other indications, traceable in France, in Germany, as well as here, betoken that a new era in the spiritual intercourse of Europe is approaching; that instead of isolated, mutually repulsive National literature, a World-Literature may one day be looked for?'

Once the light of this new dawn breaks upon the darkness of ignorance and mutual suspicion, there is no knowing into what murky corners it might not penetrate. In his introduction to the German version of Carlyle's *Life of Schiller*, Goethe alludes in prophetic tones to the political gains which Britain may yet derive from the study of German literature.

It is well enough known [he writes] that the inhabitants of the three British Kingdoms are not exactly living in the most complete harmony; that on the contrary each neighbour finds sufficient fault with the others to justify a secret aversion in his own mind. Now I am convinced that, as the knowledge of German literature, of its moral and aesthetic qualities, spreads through the triple realm of Britain, a quiet community of Germanophilists will form at the same time, who, because of their friendly feelings towards a fourth nation, so closely akin to them, will feel united and at one with each other too.

German studies in Britain as a common platform on which Englishmen, Scotsmen, and Irishmen can meet in amity—a charming thought, even if Goethe was speaking with his tongue in his cheek.

About the younger literary generation which followed the age of Goethe and Schiller in Germany, Carlyle wrote less, and on the whole with less distinction. His essay on Novalis deals almost entirely with philosophical matters, literary criticism appearing only as an occasional digression. And when it does appear it is not always of the happiest. Not many readers of *Heinrich von Ofter-dingen* would agree with Carlyle when he describes that strangely fantastic work, with its hero for ever seeking the enchantment of a dream world beyond time and space, as being written 'much in the everyday manner', or when he denies a place among its author's 'most remarkable compositions' to the book which gave the Romantic Movement the symbol of the Blue Flower.

With Zacharias Werner, August Klingemann, and Adolf Müllner Carlyle deals according to their deserts. These are easy targets— a little too easy, perhaps, for so formidable a marksman; but when (in the essay entitled *German Playwrights*) he trains his sights on Grillparzer, he proves to be sadly wide of the mark. The very first sentence of his critique—'Franz Grillparzer seems to be an Austrian'—suggests a rather haphazard approach, and what follows is no better. One has to remind oneself, of course, that some of the plays on which Grillparzer's fame as a dramatist most securely rests—*Des Meeres und der Liebe Wellen, Der Traum, ein Leben, Weh dem, der lügt!*—were not yet in existence at the time when Carlyle's essay was published (1829). Even so, such epithets as 'innocent' and 'comparatively harmless' are regrettably inadequate when applied to *König Ottokar*; and when one thinks of some of the principal characters in the play—of Ottokar, of Margarete, of Zawisch—Carlyle's comment ('certain of the *dramatis personae* are evidently meant to differ from certain others, not in dress and name only, but in nature and mode of being') seems unwarrantably supercilious. *Sappho*, too, deserved better at the hands of one who so ardently admired the author of *Tasso*: he might at least have given Grillparzer credit for having 'ploughed with Goethe's heifer'.[1] Instead he damns the play with faint praise, conceding that 'there is a degree of grace and simplicity in it, a softness, polish and general good taste, little to be expected from the author of the *Ahnfrau*', and commending Grillparzer's 'dexterity' in avoiding 'the ridicule that lies within a single step' of Sappho's situation. Although he discerns some poetic merit in the concluding scene, the drama as a whole strikes him as being 'weak and thin'. How strangely all this contrasts with Byron's extravagant praise! (Having read *Sappho* in an indifferent Italian translation, Byron recorded his impression in his diary,[2] calling the play 'superb and sublime', and its author 'a

---

[1] Cf. Grillparzer's account of his third visit to Goethe's house during his stay at Weimar in the autumn of 1826.   [2] January 12, 1821.

high intellect', 'a great and goodly writer' whose name—'a devil
of a name, to be sure, for posterity'—future generations would have
to learn to pronounce.) Very probably the blood and thunder
of *Die Ahnfrau* had created a bias in Carlyle's mind which made it
difficult for him to do justice to the other two plays. Perhaps his
critique is best viewed in the spirit in which he himself takes leave
of the fate tragedy and its unhappy ghost: 'Of this poor Ancestress
we shall only say farther: Wherever she be, *requiescat! requiescat!*'

When in 1828 Carlyle became a candidate for the Chair of Moral
Philosophy in the University of St. Andrews, he wrote to Goethe
for a testimonial, which reached him after some delay. Although
it arrived too late to prosper the application which it was intended
to support ('mustard after dinner', Carlyle observed in a letter to
his brother, 'which these rough feeders shall not so much as smell!'),
the recipient vowed to treasure it 'as a prouder document than any
patent from the Heralds' College'.[1] It contains, among other things,
a balanced summing-up of Carlyle's qualities as a critic of German
literature from the pen of Germany's greatest man of letters:

> I have had occasion to observe with pleasure Mr. Carlyle's admirably profound
> study of German literature, and have noticed with sympathy how he has not
> only succeeded in discovering the Beautiful and the Human, the Good and the
> Great in our authors, but has also freely given of himself in return, enriching us
> with the treasures of his mind. One must acknowledge that in regard to our
> writers, who combine moral with aesthetic ideals, his judgment is clear, and that
> at the same time he has views of his own, revealing thereby that what he says rests
> on an original foundation.

The parcels of books and periodicals which Carlyle received from
Goethe included the newly published Goethe-Schiller correspondence. Looking back upon the years of his friendship with Schiller,
Goethe saw that momentous decade as the zenith of his life; when-
ever he speaks of it—in his conversations with Eckermann, in his
letters, in his *Epilog zu Schillers 'Glocke'*, in his *Annals*—the nostalgic
note is unmistakable.

> Er glänzt uns vor, wie ein Komet entschwindend,
> Unendlich Licht mit seinem Licht verbindend.

Did he not preserve Schiller's last letter 'as a sacred relic' among
his treasures,[2] and did he not arrange for Schiller's remains to be
laid to rest beside his own grave? For him the Schiller years had
been 'a new spring during which everything was joyously bur-

---

[1] Letter to Goethe, April 18, 1828.
[2] J. P. Eckermann, *Gespräche mit Goethe*, January 18, 1825.

geoning';[1] 'life could not stagnate in those branches of science and art which we regarded as our own'.[2] 'However different our two natures', he remarked to Eckermann,[3] 'we were nevertheless at one in our aims, which made our relationship so close that really neither could live without the other'. He did not grudge years of meticulous editorial work in preparing his correspondence with Schiller for publication; it was to be the abiding memorial of their friendship and partnership, 'a great gift to be offered to the Germans, and indeed to mankind'.[4] In a letter to Carlyle in which he promised the early despatch of the last four volumes,[5] he said: 'May they serve you as a magic chariot to transport you into our midst at that time when whole-hearted endeavour was the order of the day, when no one thought of making claims but everyone only strove to acquire merit.' What more fitting gift could have been bestowed on the Scottish biographer of Schiller and on the critic who, in the words of George Henry Lewes, 'first taught England to appreciate Goethe'?

[1] *Tag- und Jahreshefte*, 1794 s.f.   [2] Ibid., 1799.   [3] October 7, 1827.
[4] Letter to K. F. Zelter, October 30, 1824.   [5] April 13, 1830.

INDEX

A. GENERAL

B. REFERENCES TO SCHILLER'S WORKS

PLAYS

POEMS

PROSE WRITINGS

24539
870.